**Do it The Lazy Way**
alpha books

D0506599

1. Fill your Caboodle of Fun with kid entertainment a_____ every-where you go (see Chapter 4).

2. Create a "crash corner" of pillows, blankets, and comforters so your kids can frolic away that rainy-day energy (see Chapter 11).

3. Watch your kids turn old junk into new toys in their science lab (see Chapter 12).

4. Work wonders by recycling a garage-sale trophy into a rotating award for the cleanest bedroom (see Chapter 15).

5. Set up a permanent crafts bin so your kids can craft some fun whenever they like (see Chapter 13).

 **The Lazy Way** *alpha books*

One luxurious
bubble bath

 **The Lazy Way** *alpha books*

Access to most comfortable
chair and favorite TV show

 **The Lazy Way** *alpha books*

One half-hour massage
(will need to recruit spouse, child, friend)

 **The Lazy Way** *alpha books*

Time to recline and listen to a favorite CD
(or at least one song)

cut

6. Turn family chores into giggles just by playing Job Tag (see Chapter 10).

7. Roll out endless art fun by giving your kids a newspaper end roll (see Chapter 11).

8. Whoosh up exciting fountains of foam with simple kitchen supplies (see Chapter 12).

9. Discover how pizza boxes make great toys (see Chapter 9).

10. Capture both fun and memories as your kids document their day with a disposable camera (see Chapter 6).

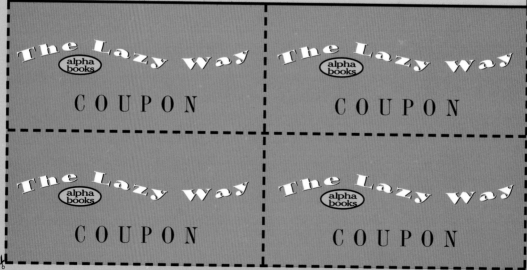

The Lazy Way
alpha books
COUPON

The Lazy Way
alpha books
COUPON

The Lazy Way
alpha books
COUPON

The Lazy Way
alpha books
COUPON

Keep Your Kids Busy

Keep Your Kids Busy

Barbara Nielsen and
Patrick Wallace

Macmillan • USA

**To our son,
Patrick Wallace**

Macmillan Publishing books may be purchased for business or sales promotional use. For information, please write to Special Markets Department, Macmillan Publishing USA, 1633 Broadway, New York, NY 10019.

International Standard Book Number: 0-02-863013-0
Library of Congress Catalog Card Number: 98-89564

02 01 00 99   4 3 2 1

Interpretation of the printing code: the rightmost number of the first series of numbers is the year of the book's printing; the rightmost number of the second series of numbers is the number of the book's printing. For example, a printing code of 98-1 shows that the first printing occurred in 1998.

Printed in the United States of America

Book Design: Madhouse Studios

Page Creation: Carrie Allen, Steve Balle-Gifford and Louis Porter, Jr.

You Don't Have to Feel Guilty Anymore!

IT'S O.K. TO DO IT *THE LAZY WAY!*

It seems every time we turn around, we're given more responsibility, more information to absorb, more places we need to go, and more numbers, dates, and names to remember. Both our bodies and our minds are already on overload. And we know what happens next—cleaning the house, balancing the checkbook, and cooking dinner get put off until "tomorrow" and eventually fall by the wayside.

So let's be frank—we're all starting to feel a bit guilty about the dirty laundry, stacks of ATM slips, and Chinese takeout. Just thinking about tackling those terrible tasks makes you exhausted, right? If only there were an easy, effortless way to get this stuff done! (And done right!)

There is—*The Lazy Way*! By providing the pain-free way to do something—including tons of shortcuts and timesaving tips, as well as lists of all the stuff you'll ever need to get it done efficiently—*The Lazy Way* series cuts through all of the time-wasting thought processes and laborious exercises. You'll discover the secrets of those who have figured out *The Lazy Way*. You'll get things done in half the time it takes the average person—and then you will sit back and smugly consider those poor suckers who haven't discovered *The Lazy Way* yet. With *The Lazy Way,* you'll learn how to put in minimal effort and get maximum results so you can devote your attention and energy to the pleasures in life!

THE LAZY WAY PROMISE

Everyone on *The Lazy Way* staff promises that, if you adopt *The Lazy Way* philosophy, you'll never break a sweat, you'll barely lift a finger, you won't put strain on your brain, and you'll have plenty of time to put up your feet. We guarantee you will find that these activities are no longer hardships, since you're doing them *The Lazy Way*. We also firmly support taking breaks and encourage rewarding yourself (we even offer our suggestions in each book!). With *The Lazy Way*, the only thing you'll be overwhelmed by is all of your newfound free time!

THE LAZY WAY SPECIAL FEATURES

Every book in our series features the following sidebars in the margins, all designed to save you time and aggravation down the road.

- **"Quick 'n' Painless"**—shortcuts that get the job done fast.
- **"You'll Thank Yourself Later"**—advice that saves time down the road.
- **"A Complete Waste of Time"**—warnings that spare countless headaches and squandered hours.
- **"If You're So Inclined"**—optional tips for moments of inspired added effort.
- **"The Lazy Way"**—rewards to make the task more pleasurable.

If you've either decided to give up altogether or have taken a strong interest in the subject, you'll find information on hiring outside help with "How to Get Someone Else to Do It" as well as further reading recommendations in "If You Really Want More, Read These." In addition, there's an only-what-you-need-to-know glossary of terms and product names ("If You Don't Know What It Means, Look Here") as well as "It's Time for Your Reward"—fun and relaxing ways to treat yourself for a job well done.

With *The Lazy Way* series, you'll find that getting the job done has never been so painless!

Series Editor
Amy Gordon

Editorial Director
Gary Krebs

Director of Creative Services
Michele Laseau

Cover Designer
Michael Freeland

Managing Editor
Robert Shuman

Development Editor
Matthew X. Kiernan

Production Editor
Faunette Johnston

What's in This Book

Do You Play Enough?

It's hard to be a parent. You're often caught between the proverbial rock and a hard place. Instead of enriching kids' lives with great activities and learning experiences, you're busy fixing that electrical switch, painting the living room, or replacing the gutters. You are forever choosing between keeping the house from going to wrack and ruin on one hand and your kids, Ruin and Rack, on the other.

That's how we felt, too.

Yet there is a solution. This book shows you how to be an exciting, idea-filled parent, even when you're busy taking care of life. Do it *The Lazy Way*!

It would make a great story if we told you that we discovered our lazy ways in a dream visitation from a favorite grandmother… or a kindly old psychotherapist. But the answer actually came from our son.

"You guys don't play enough," he said. He was right.

What's Inside

This book is divided into four parts. If you like, you can either skim through Part 1 or save it until later because it's not actually meant to be read; it's meant to be used. When you're ready, this is where you'll find useful lists of everything we think the well-prepared *Lazy Way* household ought to have.

The real fun starts with Part 2. From that point on, you'll find tons of parental tricks, sleights of hand, kid-tested games, strategies, educational activities, and more winning ways, all designed to keep your kids busy without making yourself even busier. Part 3 is divided into two sections.

First we go outside to play and then we duck back indoors. Finally, we wind everything up with some easy extras in Part 4.

You'll soon see that keeping your kids active and off the couch doesn't have to turn you into a full-time coach and activity planner—in fact, we think the best parenting method of all is *The Lazy Way*! We've packed this book with activities that foster independence and creativity precisely because they are quick, easy, and don't require heavy parental involvement. As your kids have fun playing and exploring these activities, they'll start to bubble over with their own ideas of what to do.

Now and again, we've broken out special tips under separate headings. These are ideas or activities that we've found to be particularly useful or fun—except for the ones titled "A Complete Waste of Time," which are cautionary laugh bumps intended to help you avoid unnecessary trouble or work.

Now you know enough to begin your work-saving adventure. We can feel your fingers twitching at the edge of the page. You're ready to start getting lazy.

THANK YOU

Our greatest thanks goes to our eight-year-old son, Patrick. It was he who invented Fireball Fights and lots of other delightful games and activities to be found in this book. Equally important, he listened patiently to endless dinnertime discussions about the book, the whole book, and nothing but the book. His "best old buddy, old pal," Jack Carpenter, also deserves thanks for always being ready to help with the endless testing and tinkering that went with new ideas.

Our agent, Martha Casselman, deserves our appreciative thanks for artfully getting the ball rolling (and then offering encouragement and sympathy while it rolled over us).

We are indebted to Karen Gaupp-Wozniak for generously volunteering a long ton—that's bigger than a regular ton—of absolutely terrific creative ideas she perfected with her daughter, Cala. We are also grateful to Jenny Santoro, who is a walking storehouse of kid-fun from which we borrowed liberally. Sherrilyn Sabo deserves our thanks for sharing some of those brilliant techniques we admire in her stylish, get-to-the-point kind of parenting. Pati Lanning, too, stepped forward with support and ideas whenever we needed them.

Throughout the process of researching and writing this book, we turned frequently to our dear friend, Karen Short, who was always ready with sound advice and her unique brand of clever whimsy. She serves as our personal role model for heroism.

Finally, it was a great delight to have Matthew X. Kiernan as our editor. We soon learned to look forward to his perceptive comments and intelligent suggestions and it was a comfort to know that someone was looking for meaning in all of our jokes, sometimes when there was none.

Simply Kidding Around

Are You Too Lazy to Read "Simply Kidding Around?"

1 I see some lists in this section. I've heard that "lista" is Spanish for "ready," and I don't think I am. ☐ Yes ☐ No

2 I think one of the kids is using my glasses. ☐ Yes ☐ No

3 I'm a graduate of a speed-reading course, and I've already read that part. I just haven't understood it yet. ☐ Yes ☐ No

The Easy Stuff

Your kids will have a blast once you've stocked up on the right stuff. Here in one list are all sorts of useful items to help keep kids busy—though we only mention those you might not have.

Most of the ideas, tricks, and techniques you'll learn in the following chapters make use of ordinary household items. They're probably things you and your kids have been walking past, over, or around without realizing what they really are… toys!

As you go through the checklist, you might not immediately understand the reason we've included some items, but all will become clear later on. Return to this chapter after you've read the book. These lists will serve as a convenient starting point when planning your shopping trips. Naturally, you don't have to buy everything at once! Just acquire a few items at a time as it suits your family.

FROM THE CRAFTS STORE

- Aprons, bibbed (1 per child)
- Construction paper

- Craft glue
- A hatbox. The cardboard variety is a seasonal item at most craft stores. Because you'll be creating an "heirloom," you might want to consider investing in a real hatbox. These are large cases fitted with a handy carrying handle, finished in a variety of handsome patterns and colors. Nice ones are available for around $45. Two good sources are:

  Samuel's Hats, 10 Maiden Lane, NY, NY 10038; 212-513-8788; carries a wide variety

  Tip Tops, 1140 19th St. NW, Washington, DC; 888-821-HATS; offers a small selection

- Markers, washable
- Paint cups, no-spill; if you can't find them at a craft store, call Constructive Playthings at 800-832-0572
- Paintbrushes (minimum one per child)
- Picture frames, wooden
- Pipe cleaners, multiple colors
- School glue
- Scissors; be sure to choose age-appropriate models; most stores carry a range of choices: plastic scissors for wee-little ones; short, stubby types for bigger kids; and "normal" scissors for older children with more expertise

YOU'LL THANK YOURSELF LATER

You can help prevent frustration for the lefties in your family (and younger kids who haven't settled on a hand) by buying the new scissors designed to work with either hand. They're even available at many grocery stores now.

- Scrapbook labels
- Scrapbooks (one per child)
- Tempera paint, washable
- Wooden craft sticks

FROM THE DISCOUNT STORE

- Baby wipes; get boxes for your car, your Caboodle Kit, the kitchen, and the kids' rooms
- A backpack or a small duffel bag
- Balloons of all colors, but be sure to get a bunch of large pink ones
- A bed tray with legs
- A camera, disposable (get several)
- Clothespins
- Darning needles (for adult use only)
- Fingernail polish-remover pads (presoaked)
- A magnifying glass (very powerful ones are available from Edmunds Scientific, listed in the "Stuff from Miscellaneous Sources" section)
- A mop and broom, child-size
- A photo album, small
- Photo labels
- A rain suit and rain boots for each child

QUICK PAINLESS

If you're having trouble finding reasonably priced rain suits for your little puddle jumpers, try Land's End. Call 800-356-4444 and ask for their kids' catalog.

- A thermometer, unbreakable
- Tongs or chopsticks

FROM THE GROCERY STORE

- Alum
- Baby bottles with nipples, small; these will become no-spill paint cups, so you need one for each color of paint your kids will be using (usually six will do the trick)
- Baking soda
- Corn syrup
- Cornstarch
- Drinking straws, wildly colored, if possible
- Food coloring (get lots and lots!)
- Gelatin, unflavored
- Paper bags, lunch-size
- Plastic bags, large and sealable
- Rigatoni (or other raw tube pasta)
- Sponges

FROM THE COSTUME STORE

You enter looking for plastic noses with glasses (you want at least two sets, even if you only have one child), but this is a place to have some fun. Maybe you also ought to bring back some of those vampire teeth—Hey! Get some Halloween masks!—and how about some black eye patches? That's fine with us. We'll find a way to use them.

YOU'LL THANK YOURSELF LATER

The perfect time to visit a costume store is right after Halloween. You'll find all kinds of delightful must-have's at affordable prices.

FROM THE HARDWARE STORE

- A box knife (utility knife); this tool is for adult use only, not only because the blade is very sharp, but because it is so important to keep track of just what is on the other side of the box when you cut

- Masking tape

- Packing tape; (store this where little hands cannot reach)

- ¾" plastic plumbing pipes; for your starter kit, buy four 6' lengths and cut (or have the store cut) them to yield six 2' segments and 12 1' segments

- ¾" plastic plumbing joints; for your starter kit, you need six elbows, six "T" joints, and six straight connectors

- Safety goggles (1 pair per child)

- String, heavy

- Tools, age-appropriate (to stock the kids' tinkering place)

FROM THE GARDEN-SUPPLY STORE

- Butterfly plants (zinnias, purple coneflowers, lantana)

- Caterpillar host plants (dill, parsley, fennel)

- Garden tools, child-size

- Sand (enough for a backyard sand box)

- Spray bottles

QUICK 🔲 PAINLESS

Plastic plumbing pipes and joints are inexpensive, are easy to find, and are fun for kids to play with. They are the first step to creating delightful Rube Goldberg contraptions.

FROM THE OFFICE-SUPPLY STORE

- A hole puncher
- Large rubber bands (one bag)

FROM THE BOOK STORE

- *Anti-Coloring* book series (published by Henry Holt)
- *I Spy* book series (published by Scholastic)
- A book of riddles
- *Brain Quest* cards (published by Workman)
- A children's encyclopedia (*The New Book of Knowledge* or *Children's Britannica*)
- *Field Guides* to insects, butterflies and caterpillars, and animal tracks
- A joke book

FROM THE SPORTS STORE

- Ping-Pong balls
- A stopwatch
- Tennis balls

FROM THE TOY STORE

- Bean bags
- Colored sidewalk chalk
- A set of sandbox toys (plastic sifter, etc.)
- Squirt guns (one per child)

QUICK 💿 PAINLESS

Kids love to play office, theater, or store. You can put together a terrific pretend kit at an office-supply store. Get a roll of tickets, stick-on name tags, sales receipts, telephone message pads, rubber stamps ("Cancel", "Paid"), and some pencils. Voilà!

- Travel-size board games

- A variety of boredom breakers (small, very inexpensive toys to be produced as little surprises)

- Yak Bak (if you don't already have a microcassette recorder)

FROM THE DRUGSTORE

- A box of disposable surgical gloves; (These also can be found in medical-supply stores and even home-improvement superstores—contractors know this trick, too)

- Plastic syringes (without needles)

STUFF FROM MISCELLANEOUS SOURCES

- China shop: A very special bowl, plate, and cup for sick days

- Knickknackery: Interesting chest or trunk for a costume box

- Import shop: Hand bell to sit at a sick child's bedside

- Mail order: A high-power pocket microscope (models are available starting at $10). We found ours in the Edmunds Scientific Optics catalog, available free by calling 609-573-6350

- Printer: Paper scraps from printing jobs

- Newspaper: Newspaper end roll

- Library: Library cards, one per child

IF YOU'RE SO
INCLINED

Take time to look for squirt guns, sandbox toys, and similar items at summer's end. You'll find them marked down to bargain-basement prices.

- Bank: Coin wrappers (also available—but not for free!—at office-supply stores)
- Game store: 12-sided dice (great for math practice)

STOP THROWING GOOD STUFF AWAY!

Did you know that every week you throw things into the trash that actually are pretty good tools for keeping your kids busy? Find a good spot to save a few old milk jugs and soft-drink bottles, some pie tins, and various cans and jars. You don't have to fill a room with them, just a medium-size cardboard box in the garage, perhaps. That way, they'll always be handy when needed. Here's a list of good stuff to start saving:

- Aluminum pie tins, large and small
- Cardboard boxes of all sizes
- Coffee cans and small tin cans (make sure there are no sharp edges)
- Egg cartons (and even a quart bottle full of broken eggshells!)
- Empty jars of various sizes, including two or three large ones—these aren't items for play; they're for housing critters, storing loose change, and other serious stuff

A COMPLETE WASTE OF TIME

The 3 Worst Things to Do at a Crafts Store Are:

1. Ask a clerk, "What do kids enjoy doing?" The 22-year-old (who babysat her nieces—twice) will sell you everything on aisle three and four.

2. Buy a great big pair of sharp-pointed scissors for your 3-year-old. (You don't need a joke about this.)

3. Choose a glue that does not have "Non-toxic" printed on its label. Kids eat glue. No one knows why.

- Empty matchboxes (great beds for "little guys")
- Hand-me-down clothes and accessories such as costume jewelry, gloves, scarves, big shirts, and hats or caps
- Hi-tech castoffs such as an old computer keyboard
- Interesting-looking buttons
- Margarine tubs
- Milk jugs and jug caps
- Three-liter soft-drink bottles
- Old newspapers, magazines, and catalogs
- A few old technical books with complicated-looking diagrams
- Biodegradable packing peanuts—the "meltable" kind made from vegetable starch
- Plastic bottle caps
- Broken appliances that have been rendered safe such as toasters with the cords cut off (steer clear of tube-bearing devices such as old radios or TVs)
- Scraps of nail-free lumber
- One or two shoe boxes
- Toilet-paper and paper-towel rolls—save 'em all!
- Toothpaste caps (great control buttons for kid-inspired gizmos)

Save, save, save—you've got the idea! Your reward will come in the days and months ahead as your kids dive into creative projects.

The Lazy Way

Getting Time on Your Side

	The Old Way	The Lazy Way
Wondering what kids really want	30 minutes per day	0 minutes
Wishing you owned a rubber nose with glasses	5 minutes	0 minutes
Looking for something to amuse kids for the next 15 minutes	15 minutes	1 minute
Shopping for playthings when you throw great ones away every day	90 minutes	0 minutes
Preparing a list to stock your house for fun!	55 minutes	1 minute
Hearing "I don't have anything to play with."	At least 2 times each week	0 minutes

Fast, Fun Equipment

Every kid will delight in this list of versatile "toys" that are so timelessly basic and simple, they're brilliant. Best of all, they don't need batteries.

OUTDOOR STUFF

Kids thrive outdoors, yet it still takes more than blue skies and an acre of dirt to keep them happy. That's why the prepared parent, like an astronaut, needs to have "the right stuff."

Kiddie Pool

Every spring, discount stores sell preformed plastic pools for next to nothing. You can't have a child without one of these. In fact, we think they should be handed out as you leave the hospital. If any of your kids are still under 30, buy one.

Because it can be a bit awkward getting home with a pool strapped to the roof of your car, consider cultivating a friendship with someone who drives a truck or a large van.

Of course, you might decide to buy an inflatable pool. They're a snap to get home and are more convenient to store during the winter. The bad news is that it takes a lot of

red-faced huffing and puffing to blow one up. Therefore, if you choose an inflatable pool, we recommend that you also invest in an electric pump to go with it. (Forget a hand pump or a bicycle pump. We've learned from personal experience that both are agonizingly slow and inefficient.)

After your pool is set up, be sure you are around to keep an eye on the kids when they are playing. Without supervision, a bunch of wet kids will soon show themselves to be absolute geniuses at thinking up new ways to cause disaster.

With that out of the way, here are just a few of the poolish things your kids will enjoy:

- Cooling off in the pool on a hot summer day
- Playing with water toys
- Splashing around with the family dog
- Adding bubble bath
- Making it the central reservoir for water gun battles
- Turning it into a mud hole (for the ugly details, see Chapter 6)

Tubby Stuff

Stock up on large plastic tubs the next time you find them on sale. As you'll discover in the chapters to come, they're useful for all sorts of things from outdoor water play to an indoor sandbox, a crafts bin, or even just storage containers.

The Untiring Tire Swing

If there's a big tree in your yard, you can create thousands of hours of fun by installing a tire swing. Our quick-and-dirty technique doesn't even require climbing the tree to get the rope attached!

Of course, after you've hung your rope, you don't have to just tie a tire onto it. Adding knots every 10 inches or so turns that simple rope into an excellent climbing toy for building upper-arm strength.

Here's what you will need to begin roping in the fun:

A small tire (check your favorite service station)

An electric drill

Weather-resistant rope (certified for marine use)

A weighted object

1. Look for a strong branch (at least 4 inches thick) above an area free from extruding roots or other painful-to-fall-on objects. Pay attention to the way the branch connects to the trunk. You want it to extend straight out rather than angling up like one stroke of a V. (Angled limbs tend to be weaker.) Also look out for nearby branches that are weak and likely to fall.

2. Cut off a length of rope at least twice the height of the limb you've selected. (Remember the equilateral triangle? You don't? Then just guess at the height.)

QUICK ⚬ PAINLESS

In lieu of a tire swing, you can easily make a classic rope swing by drilling a hole in a board, threading the rope through, and tying a big holding knot.

3. Tie a weighted object to one end and toss it over the branch. (You know you're going to miss the first couple of times, so get the kids out of the way lest the weight bonk them on the head.) Higher limbs might require using light string or even thread for this first stage. The thread can then be tied to the rope to pull it up and over.

4. After the rope is looped around the top of the limb, shake it along the bough using the two hanging ends until it's in the exact position you like. Make sure the rope hangs far enough away from the trunk so swinging kids won't crash into it.

5. Tie a small bowline or a lariat loop on one end, feed the other end through the loop, and pull until the rope is snug at the bough.

6. Tie on the tire at the proper height and trim off any excess rope. Drill numerous holes in the bottom of the tire to prevent rainwater from collecting inside.

A Place of Their Own

It's rare nowadays to live in a neighborhood where kids can enjoy the rich excitement of a vacant lot on which to build a fort or a tree house all their own, a hide-out where they can decide the day's adventures, spy on pretend enemies, or just hang out.

Traditionally, these were kid-made affairs, cobbled together with scrap lumber and nails. The mere fact that they stayed erect (mostly by leaning against the surrounding bushes and trees) was a source of immense pride to all involved.

If your kids are lucky enough to have access to such a hide-out, that's great. If not, your mission is to try to find space in your backyard to supply that missing fort or clubhouse. It needn't be fancy—imagination will easily make up for whatever it lacks.

If you prefer a more finished look, check in the Yellow Pages under the Playground Equipment heading or visit a large home-improvement store. There you will find forts of all kinds (or kits to build them), with features from slides and rings to rope-climbing nets. In selecting one for your family, tally up the interests of your kids. Make sure you include a basic hide-out where your crew can:

- Hold neighborhood club meetings
- Have lunch or snacks
- Stage backyard camp-outs in sleeping bags
- Pretend with friends that the fort is a sailing ship, a castle, a frontier outpost, or whatever

The Bark on Pup Tents

If you don't have space for a fort, consider a pup tent. (In fact, even if you *do* have a fort, consider a tent.) Like forts, tents are wonderful for neighborhood powwows, imaginative play, backyard camp-outs, and just hanging out. They have the added advantage, however, of being able to appear and disappear as needed.

If you're worried about struggling with tent stakes and ropes, don't. Today's small tents often are easy enough for kids to put up themselves. What's more, many of them can even be pitched indoors!

QUICK 🔲 PAINLESS

A large cardboard box easily can be converted into a great (though temporary) hide-out for kids. For the lowdown on boxes, check out Chapter 9.

One caveat, however, is that possession of a tent often creates some mild pressure from the kids to actually go camping. This can be a surprisingly blissful experience if done right, and it can be as near to Hell as the living may come if done wrong—during mosquito season, for instance. If you decide to do it, talk to experienced campers first.

Sand Fun

At every park you'll see them, bunches of little kids climbing straight into the sandbox the way ants mob a forgotten slice of birthday cake. The same timeless involvement also can happen right in your own back-yard, if you take the hint. Provide a sandbox, some toys, a little water, and some simple digging and molding tools, and your kids will stay busy for hours. Even older kids have fun with sand. They can:

▪ Try out elaborate sand sculptures from alligators to zebras. (Wet sand is darker than dry so, if you're very careful, you can dribble on the stripes.)

▪ Build ancient cities such as Machu Picchu or Angkor Wat.

▪ Create complex sand forts including battlements and moats.

▪ Dig hand-size tunnels and make extensive roadways.

QUICK ⬤ PAINLESS

To make caring for your sand a snap, cover the box with an all-weather tarp when it isn't in use. This will avoid any unpleasantness with animals or falling leaves.

INDOOR STUFF

Considering the fact that kids are born indoors and seem to spend a lot of time there, you may suppose that the standard home comes equipped with everything needed. Yet, there are a few less-than-obvious items that we think you'll find especially handy to own.

Keep Those Chins Up

A simple chinning bar on the door frame of your child's bedroom is a great way to provide an instant exercise session, especially on rainy days. The bar lifts out of two inconspicuous mounting brackets when not in use, and the whole thing is very simple to install, requiring just four screws. Check with a sports store for the different types.

Sleeping Bags

Don't worry, we really aren't trying to make you go camping. Kids just love the occasional chance to make a big adventure out of a simple thing like going to bed. No matter what the weather is like outside, letting the kids spread their bed rolls in the hall or on the living room floor sends them into paroxysms of delight. They'll spend the hours until bedtime fetching flashlights and their favorite toys or making a tent from a blanket and some chairs.

Sleeping bags also come in handy when the kids invite their friends for a sleep-over or when they are invited themselves.

YOU'LL THANK YOURSELF LATER

If your kids really enjoy their backyard camp-outs, consider giving them a compass, a set of camping dishes, and heck, even a snow-capped mountain (on a poster) the next time you're searching for a gift.

Card Table and Chairs

Consider setting up a card table just for board games and puzzles. That way, your kids won't have to clear away their fun at dinner time. When extended family visits, you'll be happy you have an extra table where all the kids can sit together while they eat.

Puzzle Caddy

Puzzle caddies are a dandy way to move a puzzle out of the way without disturbing it. You should consider getting one if you don't have space for a card table and if your kids like to build big puzzles. Check with the Spilsbury Puzzle Company at 800-772-1760.

Getting Time on Your Side

	The Old Way	The Lazy Way
Searching for the kids	20 minutes	0 minutes (They're in the fort.)
Looking for storage to hold 112 toy soldiers	10 minutes	0 minutes
Finding lost puzzle pieces	40 minutes	0 minutes
Driving kids to the pool	35 minutes	0 minutes
Figuring out arrangements for sleep-over kids	10 minutes	0 minutes
Exercising the kids to make 'em sleepy	20 minutes	0 minutes

Quick Tips for the Funny Business

Are You Too Lazy to Read "Quick Tips for the Funny Business?"

1 I can't read about quick tips until my mother-in-law finishes telling me about all her slow ones. ☐ Yes ☐ No

2 I thought I saw a chapter about... cleaning up! Now my hands are trembling so badly I can't hold the book properly. ☐ Yes ☐ No

3 In a minute! Gads, what are the kids doing? Now, where was I? Oh yes, something about reading. ☐ Yes ☐ No

Chapter three

The Playful Parent Makes a Plan

There's no sense in straining your brain at the last instant. Here are some easy ways to organize your house so your kids can make their own smiles whenever they want.

Being organized would seem to be a no-brainer, but all sorts of very brainy people fail to do it. A parent who successfully follows *The Lazy Way* is a lot like a magician. He must load his special suit pockets ahead of time if he expects to spontaneously produce rabbits later.

The perfect place to get a firsthand look at how to pre-plan the miraculous is in a nursery school. A good preschool teacher always arranges her classroom so kids aren't overwhelmed by a jumble of junk. She squirrels away craft supplies and hides puzzles and toys, pulling them out with a flourish at just the right moment. Items with perennial appeal, such as wooden building blocks, always are kept within reach so the kids can build towers every day.

Our look at organization also includes special plan-ahead ideas, such as a Little Guys Box, that will set your kids off on a course of fun.

BIN THERE, CRAFTED THAT

A wise parent will carefully size up her child to decide how much supervision is required with craft materials. This will help prevent amusing episodes such as 3-year-old Brad trying to glue his lips together or little Ashley quietly cutting paper doll outlines from her best dress. If your kids can safely handle scissors and glue, however, the day has come for a crafts bin.

Any large plastic tub will do, although it should preferably come with a cover. Some parents use a big kitchen drawer, a cardboard box, or even a set of large shopping bags. Into this, they put supplies that enable their kids to dabble in creative projects whenever the whim strikes.

To stock a crafts bin, start with basic art supplies (see Chapter 1 for a more complete list):

- Washable paint
- Washable markers
- Age-appropriate scissors
- Glitter
- School glue
- Wiggly eyes
- Pipe cleaners
- Construction paper
- Craft sticks

Then add a variety of recycled materials:

- Milk jugs

- Tin cans

- Soft-drink bottles

- Yogurt containers

- Egg cartons

- Toilet-paper rolls

- Paper-towel rolls

- Bits of ribbon and fabric

- Interesting buttons

- Clothespins and other household items

After you've stocked your bin, spend an hour or so with your kids just messing around. Glue wiggly eyes on a toilet-paper roll and add some pipe-cleaner arms. Make an alien detector from a big matchbox. Your children will soon catch on. In no time, they'll start to come up with their own ideas and will be absorbed in delightfully wacky projects—a tin-can robot? clothespin dogs?—all because you were clever enough to set up a crafts bin.

THE COSTUME BOX

Remember how you used to wobble down the hall in Mom's high heels, modeling a snazzy party dress and a string of beads? Or the fun you had with Dad's old stuff—those giant shoes, the crooked tie, and a shirt that trailed on the floor?

If you've ever watched kids rummage through a dress-up box, you know how great it can be for

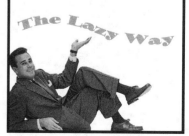

Proud of yourself for investing in bins? Pat yourself on the back by buying some clothes hooks to put near the door. Then stand back and watch as jackets and book bags levitate from the floor.

The Lazy Way

nurturing imaginative play. It's so good, in fact, that we're convinced every family should have one. Often thought of as just for girls, dress-up boxes are fabulous for boys as well, who love to swagger about in baggy suits pretending to be tough detectives. (Just call yours a costume box and high-spirited pirates like Matthew, Mike, and Tom will raid it with joy.)

To create a really fun costume box, you first need to choose an unusual container. If possible, use an interesting chest or trunk, one that hints at magic inside. In our house, a carved Chinese chest with a disabled lock does the trick. If you must use a more ordinary container, think about painting it with dramatic colors to give it a sense of mystery. The following lists provide some ideas for the treasures to be found inside.

Begin with the basics:

- Hand-me-down clothes, shoes and boots
- Old uniforms
- A dazzle of costume jewelry
- Old handbags, hats, gloves and silky scarves
- Shawls, fur stoles, and other accessories

Next add some props:

- A battered briefcase
- A broken watch
- Eyeglass frames (without the glass)
- A walking stick or light umbrella

- Wigs, from real ones to Halloween-style
- Make-up, especially eyeliner (great for making nice mustaches)

Finish up with some silly stuff:

- A plastic nose with glasses or some fake teeth
- Halloween masks
- A pair of suspenders
- Crutches or a sling
- A black eye patch

Now just sit back and watch what happens as your funny little actors paw through the goodies. From time to time, put something new in the box. When a small voice complains, "I don't know what to do," you can send it scurrying off for an hour or more just by saying, "I think there's something new in the costume box."

HOW ABOUT A SCIENCE LAB?

A tinkering spot can work wonders in keeping kids busy with inventive play. (We call ours the science lab.) We'll give you the lowdown on how to set up such a place in Chapter 12. Right now, however, you should look about for an area where you can set your kids free to tinker with batteries, magnets, and who knows what else. Some possibilities include:

- A corner of the garage
- The basement

QUICK ◎ PAINLESS

Get in the habit of checking out garage sales for dress-up items. Your kids will have fun with the odd mix you find, from a square dancer's skirt to plastic Hawaiian leis.

- A carport

- Part of your workshop

- In a pinch, a special table in the laundry room

THE FEELING BETTER BOX

The best time to assemble your family's Feeling Better Box is when everyone is perfectly healthy. Your foresight will be rewarded the next time one of your kids has to stay tucked in bed all day with a fever. We first heard about this concept when a thoughtful mother described how she had filled a fancy hatbox with treasures to be enjoyed only on sick days. The box contained:

- A miniature copy of the *Velveteen Rabbit* with its own little stuffed bunny

- A pouch jingling with foreign coins

- A decorative bottle with sweet perfume

- A book of riddles

- A snow globe with an intricate scene

- Some beautiful loose beads and yarn

- An assortment of rings, bracelets, and other costume jewelry

The idea was a big hit with our son when we tried it. We gave the concept a boyish spin by placing our treasures inside a manly plaid hatbox. We included:

- Toy soldiers to play with on the bedspread

- A pewter dragon for the soldiers to fight

- A joke book

IF YOU'RE SO INCLINED

A Rainy Day Box, like a Feeling Better Box, can lend a hint of magic to otherwise tough days. Stock yours with indoor play in mind. Some ideas include small musical instruments, a special board game, and a pair of binoculars for watching the street (especially useful for urban apartment dwellers).

- Glittering quartz rocks and shiny, polished stones
- A set of plastic vampire teeth and a hand mirror for admiring them
- A small tin stuffed with parrot feathers (donated by a friend with a parrot)
- A deck of cards
- Interesting foreign stamps and coins
- A hand bell to be rung whenever mom was needed at the bedside

Your kids will probably like their Feeling Better Box so much that they'll ask to play with it on "well" days. Take that as a compliment to your selections but be advised: to keep its allure, the box must only be placed in little hands on sick days.

THE INDOOR SANDBOX

Sometimes kids need to feel the earth between their fingers, even when it's snowing too hard to even find the sandbox, let alone dig in it. If you prepare an indoor sandbox, your kids can get down to the nitty-gritty whenever they want.

Take a large, covered plastic bin and fill it halfway with sand or cornmeal. In separate, sealable plastic bags add:

- Miniature construction vehicles
- Pennies to be buried for a treasure hunt
- Plastic dinosaurs for use in a dino dig
- Fun sandbox toys such as a sifter, cup, and funnel

A COMPLETE WASTE OF TIME

The 3 Worst Things to Do With an Indoor Sandbox Are:

1. Leave it unattended after your kids have finished playing—especially if you have a pet.

2. Fill it so high that sand storms are inevitable.

3. Allow your kids to play with it on the carpet.

Place all this in a large lawn bag and hide it in a closet until the appropriate time. When your kids are ready to play, take out the sandbox and spread the lawn bag underneath to catch any stray grains. For especially active children, tape several bags together for an extra margin of safety.

ROTATE TOYS

Follow the lead of savvy preschool teachers and rotate toys. This can be especially useful for kids who get overwhelmed by too many. (Less is actually more in fostering creative play.) Rotating toys helps reduce the clutter, and your kids will greet their old toys as "new" again. It also helps to weed through toys periodically, getting rid of those your kids have outgrown. Throw away any with broken or missing parts and set aside others for a charitable cause.

As for sentimental favorites—like a treasured doll or an old teddy bear—you can hide them safely in the attic.

THE LITTLE GUYS BOX

Many children delight in playing with miniatures, from tiny doll-house tea sets to small plastic pigs and fence rails. The Little Guys Box taps into this fascination with the tiny things in life.

To make one, start with a plastic bin and toss in small toys and other little things as you run across them. On a rainy day, you can pull out the bin and let your kids immerse themselves in the joys of creating and controlling

YOU'LL THANK YOURSELF LATER

A good time to go through your child's toys is just before a birthday or Christmas. Kids always are more willing to part with the old when they know the new is close at hand.

a miniature world. Depending on the contents, they could set up a:

- Village

- Farm

- Zoo with exotic animals

- Cozy house

- Rural landscape

- Street from the Wild West

Supply your crew with some small, clean pebbles and twigs, and they can set to work building a stone wall and a lean-to. In their hands, a small mirror becomes a pond, an empty spool of thread becomes a bedside table, and a small matchbox and cotton puffs becomes a downy bed.

Best of all for busy parents, just setting up a "little guys" world can keep your kids busy for hours.

QUICK ⬤ PAINLESS

Without telling your kids, start filling a shoe box with scrapbook items. (Use one shoe box for each child.) Toss in ticket stubs, party invitations, postcards, snapshots, and other mementos of interest. Your kids will have fun placing them in a scrapbook on the next rainy day.

Getting Time on Your Side

	The Old Way	The Lazy Way
Searching for lost scissors	15 minutes per week	0 minutes
Ordering sick kids back to bed	10 minutes	0 minutes
Racing to the kitchen for paper towels during craft time	5 frantic minutes	0 minutes
Finding your shoes, clothes, and jewelry in disarray after young actors use them	20 minutes	0 minutes
Fighting sickbed boredom	3 hours	30 minutes
Weekly psychotherapy requirements	50 minutes	0 minutes

Simple Plans for What Wasn't Planned

No matter where you are—the doctor's office, an airplane, the car, or accidentally locked in the basement—these spur-of-the-moment games will keep your kids busy and happy.

When at the doctor's office, the one thing children dread— even more than getting an injection—is waiting to get an injection. Even so, these ideas will help you turn frowns into giggles, often using nothing more than your head, which we assume you've hung onto through all the traffic jams and crowds.

THE WHOLE KIT AND CABOODLE

A good sailor wouldn't set sail without a compass, nor would a mailman march off without his mace. Likewise, *The Lazy Way* parent should never leave home without a Caboodle of Fun—a bag of goodies packed ahead of time to be produced dramatically when needed. We keep ours in the car so it's always on hand when driving to grandma's house or when facing a long wait at the dentist's.

A Caboodle of Fun can be carried around in just about anything from a backpack to a small duffel bag. Its contents will vary from family to family (you know your own kids' interests), but they should be chosen with indoor play and enclosed spaces in mind. (We recommend, for instance, that you leave out the ear-blasting trumpet and the loaded water pistols.)

Here are a few suggestions to properly complete your Caboodle:

- Washable markers
- Pencils with erasers
- A pocket-size pencil sharpener
- Drawing paper
- Small sketch pads
- *Anti-Coloring* books
- Travel-size board games
- Comic books
- Maze or activity books
- An *I Spy* book
- *Brain Quest* cards
- Action figures
- A pack of sugarless gum
- A key-ring size Magic 8 ball
- Finger puppets
- A card game such as Rat a Tat Cat

A Caboodle of Fun is enhanced if it offers kids the same element of surprise as a Christmas stocking. For that

YOU'LL THANK YOURSELF LATER

If you want to sneak in a little math practice during a road trip, include a pair of 12-sided dice in your Caboodle of Fun. Let your kids take turns rolling and adding up the numbers... while you add up the miles. The player with the most points wins.

reason, we recommend rotating the Caboodle's contents at unpredictable intervals and tossing in a few silly items to make kids giggle. Also, don't overpack or your kids will feel overwhelmed. It's far better to rotate a few Caboodle choices at a time than to present them all at once.

To get your little craftsmen started, show them how to wrap a pipe cleaner around and around a pencil. When you remove the pencil, voilà! You have created a graceful spiral. Using this basic shape as a body, your kids can twist on arms and legs, can add a head, and can accessorize with a tail, headdress, or antennae. Give them free reign and, in no time, they'll construct a pipe cleaner zoo or a tribe of really strange people.

WHAT IF?

One easy way to pass the time is to play "What if...?" with your kids. Toss out an interesting "What if...?" question and see where it leads. You might have so much fun talking about the first question that you won't need to ask anything else. Or you might make your way through a whole list of questions, stretching imaginations along the way.

Here's a short list to get you started:

- What if you could fly? What would you do?
- What if you could travel through time? Where would you go?
- What if you had a million dollars?
- What if you could live anywhere in the world? Where would you live?

Should your kids show a knack for pipe-cleaner art, reward them with a copy of *Pipe Cleaners Gone Crazy* by Klutz Press. This wonderfully wacky book presents 16 projects for kids using equipment as simple as a pencil, nail clippers, and a black marker. It even includes a pack of the "fuzzy sticks."

The Lazy Way

YOU'LL THANK YOURSELF LATER

If you find it hard to think of "What if...?" questions on the spot, write down a dozen or so on slips of paper and put them in a sandwich bag. Add this to your family's Caboodle of Fun so the questions will be handy when you need them. What if you forget them? Well, what if...

- What if you could change into an animal? Which one would you choose?

- What if everything changed color—the sky became green, the grass pink, and people blue?

- What if you could change one thing in the world? What would it be?

- What if spinach tasted like chocolate?

- What if you could talk to animals? What would you say?

- What if a genie granted you three wishes? What would you choose?

TRUTH OR LIE

Another fun conversation game is Truth or Lie. Take turns telling an anecdote that may or may not be true. The others must guess whether the statement is true. For example, a father might say, "When I was 4 years old, I had an imaginary friend named Baker. He was a blue elephant. Truth or lie?" Or a child might say, "Once I tried gluing feathers to my arms to see if I could fly. Truth or lie?" If the statement turns out to be true, the teller might want to amplify the tale. You'll be surprised by the odd tidbits you learn by playing this game. ("What? You really ate a worm?")

Once we played this game in the car and got so involved we missed our turn. Truth or lie?

LIST MAKERS

You've searched for license plates (yawn!) and played the billboard alphabet game, but now what? Last summer we whiled away some miles with an on-the-road scavenger hunt. Here's how you play:

1. Prepare a list of items your kids can search for, from a motel sign to a swamp, a barn, a bird on a wire, and a cow. (Obviously, the landscape you're traveling through will determine your choices. Leave out the swamp, for instance, if you're heading through Arizona; instead, add a saguaro cactus.)

2. The longer the list, the better!

3. As with any scavenger hunt, the person who finds the most items on the list wins.

QUICK-DRAW ARTISTS

Having a set of markers and some paper in your Caboodle is helpful, not only for casual drawing but for other activities as well. Most children enjoy the challenge of using their imagination to create something new. For instance, you might ask them to draw:

- A new spider species
- The world's best dessert
- A new playground for their school
- A garden on a different planet

Notice how the miles are gliding by? Reward your kids' good behavior by making a surprise stop for a round of ice cream cones.

The Lazy Way

- What their street would like look if they were a bird flying overhead
- How their Mom would look when seen through a fly's compound eyes
- An invention that would make their bed in the morning
- A robot friend

THE GIRL TOOK A SUITCASE TO PARIS

Waiting room magazines can be put to good use by turning them into story-telling devices. Just pick up a magazine, start at the beginning, and take turns adding to a story that connects the pictures on each page, including the ads.

Your story might go something like this:

"The girl took a suitcase to Paris. When she arrived and unpacked, she found to her surprise that the suitcase contained a fat little baby and a container of baby powder. How did the baby get there? She put on some perfume and freshened her lipstick as she pondered the problem. Perhaps she should take him to the zoo. She sat down in a soft, stuffed chair and daydreamed. Suppose the baby grew up to be a famous French chef? On the other hand, he might gamble all her money away at the casino and then run off on a sailing ship. Still, it would be fun to have a family. She could take the baby out to dine at an elegant restaurant, provided, of course, that he wouldn't dunk her cell phone into a big plate of pasta or

A COMPLETE WASTE OF TIME

The 3 Worst Things to Do With Children in a Waiting Room Are:

1. Tell them to sit quietly and read their copy of *Forbes*.

2. Let them have your car keys to play with (unless your husband's a locksmith).

3. Utter any words that can be linked through free association to "eat" or "home."

lose the keys to the luxury van. She bathed the baby in the hotel's elegant sink and later let him amuse himself licking postage stamps. No need to do anything more tonight. By tomorrow morning, he will turn into a handsome cowboy in a white hat."

And so on...

Your magazine story probably won't win any awards for its brilliant plot or characterization, but it will encourage imagination and flexible thinking and will let you have some fun with your kids.

THE KING OF TONGA

Our favorite airport game is to invent stories about the people walking by. This sometimes works in a doctor's office, too, but only if the room is large enough that people don't realize you're making up tales about them. (You also should caution your kids not to stare, even if they decide the woman near the door is an off-duty lion tamer).

Airports work best for this game because you can imagine travelers heading off to the most fantastic places. You can make your stories fanciful or realistic:

- The man in the Hawaiian shirt is the King of Tonga. He lives in a palace with a golden dome and has a pet elephant.

- That family pushing the stroller is returning from a Florida vacation. Under the blankets they've got a pet alligator.

- The woman in the black suit is a witch going to a meeting in England. Her broom is broken, so she had to take a plane.

QUICK ⬤ *PAINLESS*

- That man—the one with the briefcase—is a scientist going to Boston because he must have baked beans for his research.

- The boy with the baseball cap is a Russian spy. He's really a grownup, but he used a shrinking device to disguise himself, and he's wearing a mask to cover his mustache.

You'll be surprised how this simple exercise can make the minutes fly by, though at times you'll be tempted to stop a complete stranger and quiz him about his life. ("Aw, you mean you're not heading off to the jungle to stop an epidemic? And you don't have pickled frogs stuffed with pimento in your briefcase?")

MORE IDLE THINKING

Another play-anywhere game is to choose an ordinary object from your immediate environment—a shoe, a pencil, a chair—and then brainstorm what an alien might think it was used for (silliness is allowed). A shoe might make a good flower pot, a pencil might be a tasty between-meals snack, and a plastic chair might appear to be an outdoor sculpture.

BRAINSTORM!

Pass out a pencil and a pad to each of your kids and give them five minutes to jot down every use they can think of for the object you've chosen. When the five minutes are up, tally each list, declare the person with the longest list the winner, and then read the ideas out loud.

Have your kids vote on the funniest, wisest, weirdest, and so on.

You can play this game until you run out of objects... or until the nurse finally calls your name.

PAPER, SCISSORS, ROCK

When was the last time you saw anyone playing this fast-paced game, designed for two to three players? Do you even remember the rules? Here's what to do:

1. To begin, all players hide a hand behind their backs and make one of three symbols: scissors (a fist with two fingers in a "V"), paper (hand held flat, palm down), or rock (a fist).

2. At the count of three, the players must show their choice.

3. To determine the winner of each round, remember that scissors cut paper, rock smashes scissors, and paper wraps rock.

4. The faster you play, the more fun you'll have—and you can keep track of the rounds or not.

UPSIDE-DOWN

The next time you're sitting in a waiting room, have your child lean back, look up, and imagine the room is upside-down and she's walking on the ceiling. Most kids get a kick out of thinking about how they'd have to climb over the door frame or step across vents. It's also fun for them to embark on an imaginary walk down the hall, passing

IF YOU'RE SO
INCLINED

The book *Children's Traditional Games* by Judy Sierra and Robert Kaminski covers games from 137 countries and cultures around the world including the Japanese version of Paper, Scissors, Rock (Jan Ken Po). You'll find it fun to keep a copy handy.

light fixtures that could serve as little tables or sprinkler devices that could be silver toadstools.

THE MEMORY HAS IT

How good is your child's memory? Challenge him to look at something, look away, and then try to remember everything he saw. Keep score by counting the number of details he was able to recount. But for heavens sake, don't let him know that this mental exercise is actually good for him.

Getting Time on Your Side

	The Old Way	The Lazy Way
Number of times you said, "Come back here and sit down!"	5	0
Number of times you enjoyed leafing through a 2-year-old copy of *Time*	0	Always!
Angry looks from fellow patients	3	1 (There's always one!)
Number of times you heard, "When are we going to get there?"	12	4
Number of times you felt bored while driving (per 100 miles)	1	0
Squabbles in the back seat (per 100 miles)	4	1 (There's always one!)

A Neat End to So Much Frivolity

We've worked and slaved so you won't have to! The tips in this chapter should help you and your kids lead a simpler, neater life. After we've helped you through this transformation, we'll show you how to prevent more than a few accidents and how to clean up the ones you can't prevent in a snap.

THE WAR ON CLUTTER BEGINS

The first step toward a clutter-free home is to set aside at least one room as a toy-free zone. If a child breaks this rule, confiscate the offending toy and put it in jail for a week. Your kids will soon figure out that, well, you mean it.

Ah, isn't it wonderful to sink into a chair without having to worry that you'll squish a Barbie?

Here are some other suggestions for making your home a calm and restful place:

▥ Don't let the kids have breakfast until they have made their bed, pulled on their clothes, and put their PJs away. You'll be surprised how quickly everyone falls into the habit.

▥ Love to come home to a clean house? Before leaving to run errands, spend 5 or 10 minutes picking up.

▥ Put flowers in a vase to lift your spirits. (What was that about the kids eating the daisies?)

▥ Every night, have your little hooligans spend 10 minutes cleaning up before bedtime. Remind everyone that it's much easier to do a little work at a time than to do a whole bunch at once.

▥ Buy a whistle… or a trumpet. When play starts to get out of hand and is creating a nerve-wracking mess, instead of blowing your top, blow your whistle! That's the signal for everyone to launch into a whirlwind 10-minute cleanup session. Set the timer and make periodic announcements about how much time is left.

▥ Set up a job chart for your kids and rotate chores. If you live in a one-child household, include Mom and Dad on the roster.

▥ As suggested in Chapter 3, use large plastic bins to store craft supplies, building blocks, toy cars, or whatever. This makes picking up as easy as tossing stuff into a bin.

▥ If your kids use far too many glasses and cups, give them the job of doing the dishes for a couple of days. Stand back and watch in amazement as the number of dirty glasses shrinks to an all-time low. Repeat as needed.

- Baby wipes are invaluable for quick cleanups. Keep them in the glove compartment of your car, in your gardening-tool caddy, in the crafts bin, and in other places where they might be useful.

- If you struggle to find time to balance your check-book, to pay bills, or to write out Christmas cards, try this technique: sit down and do *your* homework while the kids do theirs.

- One clever mother we know has had her sons clean the hall toilet once a week since they were 6 or 7 years old. They don't have to clean any other part of the bathroom, however, because her aim was merely to make sure the boys improved theirs.

CRAFT OF CLEANLINESS

It's a truism that messy aftermaths go hand-in-hand with kids having fun. Paint, spills, glue, and sticky hands are all a part of childhood. Lazy parents don't mind that, but we do like to keep a few spill-stopping tricks up our sleeves, even at the risk of having our elbows look suspiciously lumpy.

Of course, we've all learned to spread newspapers on the table before uncapping the finger paints, but here are some other ways to make "*après*" art" scrub-downs as simple as *un, deux, trois* (pardon our French).

IF YOU'RE SO
INCLINED

Grungy bathroom sinks can become a thing of the past by putting a roll of paper towels in the cupboard underneath. Show your kids how to wipe the sink clean after each and every use.

Protecting Clothes and Hands

■ When your child is working with paint, glue, or other messy materials, make an instant smock by cutting arm and head holes in a plastic lawn bag. When the craft project is over, remove (and toss) the smock, revealing the astonishingly clean child underneath.

■ If you use plastic bags as smocks, keep in mind that young children must always be supervised.

■ Another option is to have a special "arts and crafts" T-shirt for your young artist. Choose a shirt large enough to cover her clothes.

■ Don't forget dad's old white dress shirts. Minus the tie, they make a perfect smock.

■ As for hands, have your child wear disposable surgical gloves (get the "extra small" size) when working on really messy crafts. With gloves, you don't have to worry about hand stains, sticky fingers, or gunk under the fingernails. Best of all, cleanup is as fast as finding a trash can.

Subdue That Glue

■ Buy some plastic syringes (without needles) from the drugstore to minimize the mess when working with glue. Your child can more precisely apply glue when squeezing it from a syringe. Used applicators can be either tossed or rinsed clean with hot water, provided you don't wait for the glue inside to dry.

- Show your kids how to use small dots of glue around the edges of the object they're gluing. Large objects also might need a dot or two in the center to keep them from bulging up. If you use dots in this way, excess glue is less likely to be squished out when the kids press their paper, doily, or feather into place.

- Let older kids use craft glue instead of school glue. It's stickier and creates less of a mess.

Easy Paint Restraint

- Have your kids mix their paint colors in the convenient cells of an empty egg carton. You then can just throw it away when they're through.

- Baby-food jars work well for storing paint colors your kids have mixed.

- To prevent spills, you can buy some of the handy, no-spill paint cups available from Constructive Playthings (800-832-0572) or from many local art-supply stores.

- You can make your own no-spill container for paint using a baby bottle with a nipple. Nip off just enough of the nipple to open a hole that fits snugly around a paintbrush. Put the nipple on inverted. Pour about an inch of paint in the jar—it can't spill out!

- Teach your kids how to dip the paintbrush hairs only halfway into the paint for easier cleanup and, incidentally, better artistic control.

YOU'LL THANK YOURSELF LATER

Train yourself to always look for the magic word, *washable*, when buying markers and paints. One moment of forgetfulness might result in a permanent reminder on the living room wall.

To avoid stiff, useless paintbrushes, remind your kids to wash them after each use. Also explain that they should store clean brushes bristle-side up.

Fingernail polish-remover pads are great for cleaning up paint. Use them to quickly erase spots from furniture, your child, or even a mistake in an art project. (After you've removed the paint, remove the remover with a cotton ball dipped in water.)

Other Simple Salvations

Your kids can cut down on the mess from glitter or sand art by folding a large piece of paper in half, unfolding it, and then placing it under their work. The paper will catch the excess grains, which you or your child can then pour back into the container by carefully lifting the paper edges to trap the grains in the crease.

Have your kids work on the driveway, in the garage, or under the carport if you think the mess will likely get out of hand.

Keep sponges, paper towels, and cleaning supplies within quick reach.

Although messes should be cleaned up by "them that made 'em," this doesn't mean little hands can't have help. The quickest way to restore order is for everyone to pitch in (yes, even you). Tackle the job right away and the mess will quickly be gone.

Teach kids the habit of cleaning up as they go, just as all the great chefs do when cooking. Most craft disasters happen when an elbow meets a paint jar that was carelessly set aside or an arm sticks to an overlooked drip of glue on the protective paper.

- Maintain your sense of humor. These little spills are nothing. You'll realize that when your child begins practicing the violin.

AVOIDING CHAOS IN THE KITCHEN

It's fun to cook with kids (see Chapter 16). Nevertheless, there are many things you can spill in a kitchen—and we all know that, if you bring kids into direct contact with anything that can be spilled, it will be. (Physicists have yet to account for the way entropy increases in the immediate vicinity of a kid.)

Still, *The Lazy Way* parent can do a few easy things to reduce the time spent wiping up:

- Use really big bowls. If a recipe calls for 4 cups, pull out a giant bowl that could hold 8 cups. This does a lot to minimize splashes when pouring or stirring.
- Bring bowls and ingredients to a child-size (or at least low) table where young kids can work comfortably and safely instead of teetering on stools at the kitchen counter.
- If an ingredient comes in a large, heavy container (such as a gallon of milk) or a "problem" container (such as a paper bag of sugar), pour a smaller quantity into a container the kids can handle more easily and safely. You'll have fewer spills if kids pour milk from a pitcher and sugar from a small, rigid container.
- Place damp towels or washcloths under the bowls kids use for stirring. The added friction makes it easier for them to keep the bowl from sliding out of their control.

YOU'LL THANK YOURSELF LATER

Give every child his own bibbed apron. This not only shields clothes from flour and chocolate smudges, it makes the kids feel like real chefs.

- Put down a large serving tray or a big cookie sheet where a small child will be working. The lip on the tray helps contain any spills, and it's easier to dump out a tray than to mop up a mess.

- Spread five or six sheets of newspaper where kids will be working. It helps speed cleanup and protects work surfaces (and your ears) from the occasional bang, clunk, and clank.

- If an older child will be using a stool, make sure it has been properly unfolded and is both sturdy and wobble-free.

- Avoid giving kids tasks for which they aren't physically or mentally ready. It could be unsafe, it probably will result in a spill, and it is certain to cause unhappy frustration.

- Finally, remember that anything involving flour will require a major cleanup. Be prepared—and have your camera ready!

OUTSIDE PLAY

Believe it or not, now and then we meet parents who try to keep their kids from getting dirty when they go outside to play. Should they succeed at all, it's only at the price of misery because getting dirty is what little children do. They have that talent, and you cannot thumb your nose at an instinct crafted by a million years of evolution. For those few parents, let us state the obvious: When you send your kids outside to play, put them in old clothes and let them have fun! Bleach, stain sticks, and iron-on patches can undo most of the damage.

- Younger kids don't mind shedding their mud-caked clothes at the back steps or on the mud porch and then padding straight to the tub. (If they are really dirty, first suggest a fun detour to the garden hose.)

- Some parents cope with dirt Japanese-style: They require their kids to take off their shoes at the door. In fact, this is the only defense against certain high-priced sneakers that leave tarry skid marks all over wood or tile floors.

- If you let your kids wear their shoes inside, make sure you invest in a mud rail and a good doormat (and teach your kids how to use these items).

- As with art projects, a lawn-bag smock can make outdoor play with mud, shaving cream, and other gooey stuff less messy.

- Teach your kids to rinse—especially grubby hands—at an outdoor faucet before heading inside.

- Remind your kids to dump sand from shoes and frogs from pockets—outside!

- Should your young ones forgetfully track in dirt, have them clean it up with the child-size mop or broom you thoughtfully purchased ahead of time.

YOU'LL THANK YOURSELF LATER

Most kids will remember to shed their shoes at the door if you place some comfy slippers within reach.

Getting Time on Your Side

	The Old Way	The Lazy Way
Time spent scrubbing up spills	10 minutes	2 minutes
Time spent getting glue off the chair seats	5 minutes	0 minutes
Time spent mopping up tracks	3 minutes	0 minutes
Time spent vacuuming up glitter	6 minutes	0 minutes
Time spent getting paint off the kitchen tile	10 minutes	0 minutes
Number of laundry loads after a big art project	2	0 minutes

Part 3

Fun for All and All for Fun

Easy Outs for Outside

Are You Too Lazy to Read "Easy Outs for Outside?"

1 You mean, they go *outside* sometimes? ☐ Yes ☐ No

2 I'd like to read it, but I can't see the letters very well through the black crayon, and I'm not sure I've found all the pages. ☐ Yes ☐ No

3 No, thank you. I'm still horrified that they got smudges on their little suits when Nanny let them outside last spring. ☐ Yes ☐ No

Chapter six

Sunny Days

In an instant, your kids can be busy exploring nature, slopping about in suds, or locating leprechauns while you enjoy a few peaceful minutes to yourself.

You'll find there is nothing sweeter than the sound of giggles faintly wafting through the window. This is what *Lazy Way* parenting is all about. It sure beats the sound of distant gunfire coming from a television set.

Here are some of our favorite ways to keep kids busy on carefree days.

CHEAP THRILLS

A simple can of shaving cream is jam-packed with instant, sweet-smelling fun. Your kids will jump at the chance to squirt out mounds of creamy white foam. They'll squish it and mash it, whip it and smash it, scoop it into summer snowballs, and even shave with it. Of course, you'll need to remind your exuberant crew not to eat it, spray it in their eyes, or squirt it in a sibling's mouth.

You'll need:

A can of shaving cream

Kitchen utensils such as potato mashers, whisks, big spoons, rotary beaters, or spatulas

Small plastic cars or action figures

Wooden craft sticks

A hand mirror

A garden hose

1. Select a good outdoor play area such as the back steps or a backyard picnic table.

2. Give your kids the can of shaving cream and show them how to shake it and squirt it. (Younger children, of course, should always be supervised.)

3. Give your kids the kitchen utensils and let them stir and smash away. Also put out the small plastic cars or figures so the kids can play with them in a snowy, mountainous landscape.

4. Boys especially enjoy pretending to shave. Tell them they can lather their faces with foam and then shave it off with the help of a hand mirror and a craft-stick razor.

5. If no one has thought of it yet, pick up a blob and... splat! (Better run away fast, though.)

6. When all the foam has gone flat, cleanup is quick and easy with a garden hose.

IF YOU'RE SO
INCLINED

A few drops of food coloring can turn snowy drifts of shaving cream into fabulous blue or pink mounds. Some kids like to rub it all over themselves to become foam monsters. Capture this tender moment on film. It's not every day your child looks like a half-melted green marshmallow. Aargh!

QUICK TUB O' SUDS

A big plastic tub filled with sudsy water can hold excitement for the younger set on a scorching summer day. Chubby little hands plunge right into the action. They pour water and slosh suds with cups and funnels, guide wobbly boats past bubble mountains, and fish for small toys hidden under the froth. You'll need:

A large plastic tub or wading pool

Mild dish-washing soap

A garden hose

Plastic cups or margarine tubs, funnels, basters, and other pouring containers

Small plastic toys

Toy boats

1. Set the tub outside where the overflow is least likely to create a muddy mess.

2. Squirt in some dish-washing soap.

3. Turn on a garden hose full blast to fill the tub with billowing bubbles.

4. Set out toys and pouring supplies and let the fun begin. (Be sure to supervise little kids whenever they are around water.)

5. After the day's adventures have ended, have your kids create a titanic tsunami by dumping the water onto the grass. (They can make this even more

A COMPLETE WASTE OF TIME

The 3 Worst Things to Do With a Tub of Sudsy Water Are:

1. Let your kids try to bring the cat into the tub with them.

2. Set the tub on a grass-free area—unless you're intentionally making a mud hole (see the section "Mudder's Day Out" later in this chapter).

3. Accidentally call the water "bath water" or the tub a "bathtub." All the fun will cease immediately.

Kids' sunscreens now come in colors from purple to blue. Buy this kind and your kids will eagerly rub the stuff on.

exciting by arranging a tableau of cars and figures to be swept away by the tide.)

A Day at the Beach

All children love going to the beach... even if it's just pretend. You'll need:

A bathing suit for each child

Sunscreen

Sunglasses for each child

A beach towel for each child

Drinks and snacks

A portable radio

A sprinkler or garden hose

1. Have your kids dress in their bathing suits and then slather on the sunscreen.

2. Spread beach towels on the lawn, set out drinks and snacks, and turn the radio to a lively station—just like a day at the shore.

3. Let your kids sunbathe, talk, and munch their snacks until they're ready to run through the sprinkler or play with the garden hose.

4. Water limbo, anyone?

MUDDER'S DAY OUT

You just can't get enough mud when you're under the age of 12. Sure, now and then a kid can be talked into standing around looking like a shrink-wrapped Barbie, but a well-rounded childhood absolutely requires getting good and grubby periodically. Ah, the pleasures of kneading, patting, pounding, and shaping mud, glorious mud!

   If you don't have a mud hole in your backyard (you don't!?), you can quickly and easily create a temporary one. For mud-pie fun, you'll need:

   Old clothes for your kids

   A large, shallow tub

   Dirt (or buy a bag of potting soil)

   Water

   Big spoons

   Aluminum pie tins, small and large

   Plastic knives

   A rolling pin

   Pebbles, flowers, twigs, leaves, and other decora-
      tions (let your kids find these)

   A garden hose or a watering can

1. Have your kids change into old clothes.

2. Put some dirt in the tub.

YOU'LL THANK YOURSELF LATER

Pick up two rolls of pennies the next time you're at the bank. On a day when you sense gathering clouds of boredom, line up your kids and yell "Scraaaaamble!" as you shower fistfuls of copper in wide, twinkling arcs across the grass.

3. Add a small amount of water and ask a little helper to mix and stir. Keep adding water slowly until the mud is deliciously sticky and gooey. If you accidentally add too much water, simply add more dirt.

4. Put out the cooking equipment and decorations.

5. Set your kids loose to make crooked mud huts and castles, funny faces in squished mud "dough," lumpy swamp creatures, primitive sculptures, and, of course, delicious gourmet mud pies.

6. Leave the finished goodies in full sun to bake until done.

7. When the messy fun is over, you can either leave the mud for future play (including plain old squishing between the toes) or empty it into a garden bed and rinse out the tub with a hose.

8. As for your mud monsters, hose them off before they go inside. Remember that they're washable—and so are their clothes.

CHALK UP SOME FAST FUN

Colored sidewalk chalk can be used for more than hopscotch grids and other games. All you need for a sidewalk art show is a few child-artists and some colored chalk. (Well, you also need a sidewalk.)

If the kids need help getting started, have them copy a picture from a book of art masterpieces or even from one of their favorite comic books. Otherwise, let them happily create their own colorful designs.

QUICK ⬛ PAINLESS

After your kids finish their sidewalk masterpieces, suggest that they draw an elaborate racetrack for use with their toy cars. They also could challenge each other with chalk mazes.

If you live in an area where many people walk by, have your kids put out a hat for donations. Naturally, you'll be the first to pitch in.

LEAPIN' LEPRECHAUNS

Though we seldom take the time to observe them, our lawns and flower beds are alive with little creatures from beetles to bumblebees. Most kids delight in picturing themselves as a tiny insect on patrol in a garden rain forest or as a playful leprechaun cavorting in the ferns. You'll need:

A flower bed or lawn

A hula hoop (optional)

1. Ask your child if he'd like to take a peek inside one of the tiny worlds that exist inside our big one. If you have a flower bed, ask him to kneel down next to it. You also could just toss a hula hoop onto the lawn. Announce that an entire miniature world is hidden there, with hundreds of bizarre insects coming and going.

2. After he's spotted a few, ask him to choose the one he'd like to be, such as a ladybug or a busy ant. If that doesn't seem to interest him, suggest that he imagine himself as a tiny leprechaun riding on the ladybug's back.

3. Ask your child to picture how the garden would look from this new perspective. A leaf might seem like a giant umbrella. A dragonfly might zoom into view like a huge, frightful beast.

QUICK ⬤ PAINLESS

The next time the kids "have nothing to do," grab an old blanket, throw it across two chairs, and invite the kids to go camping. As you walk away, say "Watch out for the bears."

4. Have your child imagine what it would be like to make his way—in tiny mode—through this towering jungle. Whoa! Watch out for that huge raindrop!

CHILD'S-EYE VIEW

Curious about how your child sees the world? Here's an easy way to gain a unique perspective. You'll need:

A disposable camera

A small photo album

Photo labels

A pen

1. Give your child a disposable camera and show her how to operate it.

2. Encourage her to go outside and take pictures of whatever she likes—her favorite places, favorite neighbors, and so on.

3. After she's filled the roll, take the film to be developed.

4. Let your child arrange the pictures in a photo album and write captions for each one. (From experience, we can tell you that the captions are important. They offer vital clues about the artist's intentions.)

5. Peruse the album together. You'll probably be surprised by some of the shots. When our son was 5 years old, for example, he documented a big ant hill, a telephone wire where a bird once sat, and a friend's scraped elbow.

POTIONS

Kids can have hours of outdoor fun with a box of food coloring and some water. They can:

- Add a few squirts of blue to a tub of water to make a gorgeous sea for their boats.
- Pretend to be magicians who can turn jars of ordinary water into sparkling, sunlit potions in blue, green, yellow, and red.
- Perform mad experiments by mixing colors (blue added to red, for example, makes purple).
- Stir up a deadly black brew by swirling all the beautiful colors into a single bowl of water while cackling like a witch.

THE ANTS GO MARCHING

Ants toil just about everywhere and are always fun to study. Remember getting down on your hands and knees to watch a team of ants struggling to lug a dead insect home to their hill? To help encourage your kids to make time for ants, all you need are some large and small crumbs. Here's what to do:

1. Send your little scouts out to find an ant trail or an ant hill.

2. When they return with a report of success, give them the crumbs and tell them to drop a few of the small ones near the ants and watch what happens.

3. After the small crumbs attract a crowd, your kids can drop the large crumbs and enjoy the fun as the worker ants struggle to carry away the loot.

QUICK ● PAINLESS

A child with an interest in insects might want to go on a bug hunt. How many different kinds of bugs can he find in the yard or neighborhood?

A BUTTERFLY GARDEN

Inviting butterflies to your garden is as simple as planting nectar-producing flowers and some host plants for caterpillars. A flower bed with clouds of fluttering butterflies is a magnet for kids. (Truth be told, though, most kids find watching the big, fat caterpillars even more enthralling.) You'll need:

Good soil

A shovel

Butterfly plants such as lantana, black-eyed susans, zinnias, or purple cone flowers

Host plants such as fennel, parsley, and dill

Water

A butterfly and/or caterpillar field guide (optional)

1. In spring or early summer, choose a 5- to 10-foot-long bed in a sunny spot with good drainage.

2. Plant a mixture of nectar-producing butterfly plants and caterpillar host plants.

3. In the days and weeks to come, remind your kids to check for caterpillars on the host plants. They'll get a kick out of watching them greedily munch the leaves and become enormously fat.

4. Bring a chrysalis inside in a ventilated jar so you and your young naturalists can watch the butterfly emerge.

IF YOU'RE SO INCLINED

Give your kids a field guide to butterflies and caterpillars. They can thumb through the pages to see which ones they've attracted.

5. After the newly emerged butterfly's wings have dried, let the kids release it in the garden.

6. Throughout the summer, you and your kids will have fun watching the happy-go-lucky flight patterns of visiting butterflies.

Congratulations! Your kids have been busy for hours without once turning on the TV. How about a big adventure as a reward? It's as close as the nearest bus, where you and your intrepid crew can go exploring all the way to the end of the line.

The Lazy Way

Getting Time on Your Side

	The Old Way	The Lazy Way
Average giggles per hour	1	4
Tubes of suntan lotion per month	1	4
Number of times you hear "This has been the best day of my life."	Huh?	3-4 per summer
Number of butterflies you and the kids can identify	0	2 (at least!)
Average tread depth on your kids' tennis shoes at the end of summer	1/4 inch	0
Brain cells destroyed by television	38,317	2 (and the set was off!)

Fast Forward Through Rain and Snow

Use these simple tricks to create boisterous outdoor fun when the temperature's right but the rest of the weather isn't.

Like postmen, neither snow, nor rain, nor heat, nor gloom of night shall keep kids from their appointed running around. Well, maybe gloom of night. If you've provided your children with warm clothing and sturdy, waterproof boots, however, there's no reason they can't go outside and brave a bit of weather. It's *The Lazy Way*, and they love it!

RAINY-DAY PLAY

For a rare treat, if it's raining hard but there's no thunder or lightning, let your kids out to play in a rain suit and boots. It's a sensory experience they'll never forget—wind-driven droplets prickling their back, the downpour drumming on their head, and the sweet smell of water fresh from the clouds. A *Lazy Way* parent can stand at the window and watch them slosh through backyard puddles, dash through wind and pelting rain, and wade in little rivers that swirl away down the driveway toward the drain. Here are some recommendations for the best rain adventures:

- Suggest that your kids whoop it up with a wild, backyard rain dance. (If you live in the country—as one of us did as a child—we can say with confidence that this is most fun when stark naked and painted with watercolors.)

- After the rain slows, let them float sticks down the gutter as they imagine themselves on board and about to be swept into a torrential underworld and then out to sea. (If you live on a busy thoroughfare, move this activity to a side street and supervise to be sure the kids stay safely on the sidewalk.)

- Have your kids try to build a beaver dam in a ditch or a backyard puddle. Just gathering sticks for the project will keep your little ones busy for at least half an hour.

- Join your kids on a walk. You, too, can revel in the unleashed fury of the storm.

Bepuddled Scientists

When the rain finally stops, kids are left with a watery world to explore. They can hurl rocks into puddles to make a big splash, can venture into ditches to hunt for water bugs, and can float toy boats in temporary ponds.

Flushed and happy after a rainy-day walk with your kids? Top off your excursion with a round of hot cocoa.

The Lazy Way

They also can enjoy a little puddle-prodding experimentation. You'll need:

Rain boots for each child

A ruler

An unbreakable thermometer

A notepad

A pen

1. Pile outside with your crew to find some handy puddles.

2. To determine the puddle's depth at its deepest point, your little scientists can measure the highest watermark on their wading boots (if they remembered not to splash around too much). Otherwise, they can insert the ruler directly into the water.

3. Have them record the data in their notepad. (Be sure to hold the notepads for them while they wade in the water. If you don't, the odds are high that every page will emerge too wet to write on!)

4. Next the kids should check the temperature of the water and record the data.

5. Return to the puddles in the days (or hours) to come. Are they getting smaller? warmer? colder?

6. Do any of the puddles have tadpoles?

QUICK PAINLESS

Very small children might not care about measuring puddles, but they'll be fascinated to watch them shrink, and shrink, and shrink. Pay a visit to a single puddle every day until it disappears.

Curious about what kind of tadpoles you've collected? A field guide to amphibians will show you and your kids the different kinds.

Raisin' Tadpoles

If your kids find some tadpoles in a puddle, why not bring a few home in a jar and watch them turn into frogs? You'll need:

A jar or a glass container

Some puddle water

Scraps of lettuce

Dechlorinating drops (optional)

A pie plate

Sloping rocks

1. Scoop up two or three tadpoles and some puddle water in a medium-size jar. Fill the water at least halfway. Be careful not to overstock with tadpoles.

2. Let your children feed the young amphibians scraps of lettuce, which will partially rot in the water.

3. As the puddle water evaporates, add dechlorinated tap water. Water can be dechlorinated either by letting it stand uncovered overnight or by using dechlorinating drops, which are available from any pet store. (Chlorine is lethal to tadpoles.)

4. After the tadpoles develop legs, transfer the puddle water to a pie plate with sloping rocks for the young frogs to climb on. When they emerge from the water, turn them lose outside.

Mud Fun

Good old mud. What child doesn't love it? Chapter 6 showed you how to create your own mud hole and let your kids plunge right in for mucky, squishy fun.

After a good rain, kids usually find their own mud spots. Send them outdoors in old clothes and boots and give them a few kitchen supplies and plastic toys. They might want to:

- Practice water engineering by building dams or by digging a miniature Panama Canal

- Make a mud pizza in an old pizza pan and garnish it with "pepperoni" rocks

- Slap together a stack of mud pancakes

- Stage plastic dinosaur wars in a muddy swamp

- Smooth out the mud with a rolling pin and play a mucky game of tic-tac-toe

- Make miniature mud snowmen and decorate them with twigs and pebbles

- Build roadways for small cars that wind past twig huts and over mud mountains

The Humble Worm

Now that we're on the subject of mud, why not move on to worms? (Why are you squirming?) Most kids find worms simply fascinating. (Keep reminding yourself that

A COMPLETE WASTE OF TIME

The 3 Worst Things To Do When It's Raining Are:

1. Forget to check shoes as the kids head outside... they'll be in their Sunday best.

2. Forget to check shoes as the kids head inside... you'll be cleaning until next Sunday.

3. Comfort a moping kid with the thought that the garden needs the rain.

they're great for the garden.) To make a worm farm, you'll need:

A three-liter soft-drink bottle

Sturdy scissors (for adult use only)

An ice pick or a finishing nail and hammer (for adult use only)

An aluminum pie plate

Two sheets of newspaper

Water

A big spoon

Dirt

Wiggly worms (let your kids hunt for them)

Food scraps such as lettuce, apple peels, and cracker crumbs

1. Cut the top off the soft-drink bottle with a sturdy pair of scissors.

2. Using the ice pick, poke some holes in the bottom of the bottle.

3. Place the bottle on the aluminum pie plate.

4. Have your kids tear the newspaper into long strips.

5. Put the strips into the bottle.

6. Add enough water to dampen the paper.

7. Mash up the newspaper with the spoon.

8. Add dirt, stir it with the newspaper, and then add more water. The mixture should be damp, not wringing wet.

9. Let your kids introduce the worms to their new home.

10. Show the kids how to bury food scraps below the surface for their lowly pets.

11. In the days to come, lightly mist the paper mix as necessary.

12. Keep your worm farm going until the kids lose interest. Then return the worms to the garden, along with the contents of their home.

LET IT SNOW, LET IT SNOW...

Frosty the Snowman and his carrot nose are a staple in many snow-covered yards, but why not step beyond that regular old schmo to make a crew of funny snow guys with their pets? You'll need:

Snow (of course!)

An aluminum pie plate

Sturdy scissors (for adult use only)

Twigs

Hair curlers (optional)

Milk-jug caps

Small potatoes

Raisins

Sticks

Spatulas, spoons, and other kitchen utensils

Quirky clothes and accessories

Spray bottles

Water

Food coloring

YOU'LL THANK YOURSELF LATER

Clothes make the man... er, snowman. Let your kids raid closets and the costume box for odds and ends—from a funky shawl to a safari hat.

1. Begin by making some basic snowman bodies.

2. Cut an aluminum pie plate in half with a sturdy pair of scissors. Scrunch the halves into each side of the snowman's head and pack snow around them to make huge ears.

3. Make funny-looking hair by sticking a thicket of small twigs in the top of the snowman's head (or use bright plastic curlers for a snow mom).

4. Use the caps of milk jugs for eyes, a funky potato for a nose, and some molded snow tinted with red food coloring for lips. (If watered down, the food coloring can add some life to those pale cheeks, too). You also can play around with arranging the features Picasso-style.

5. Add stick arms or, with the structural help of a row of twigs poked into the snowman's belly, mold a set of folded arms from snow. If you make snow arms, use kitchen utensils to smooth the packed snow.

6. Now accessorize! Try an old bathrobe and a pair of slippers, a Hawaiian shirt and sunglasses, or snorkeling gear and fins.

Snow Pets

Your kids will enjoy giving their snow people some pets. For this, you can use the same techniques and materials previously listed, plus pet accessories such as a leash and a food bowl. Here are some suggestions:

IF YOU'RE SO
INCLINED

If your children have made some Picasso-style snowmen, suggest that they use spray bottles filled with colored water to paint each side of the face a different color.

- A snow poodle with pompoms
- A calico cat (Use the spray bottle to make the different colors)
- A giant green caterpillar with a row of stick legs and twig antenna—put it on a leash held by a snowman to turn some heads
- A snow walrus with icicle tusks
- A pink snow pig

For the Birds

Setting out food for the birds can be extra fun if you put the treats on an outdoor Christmas tree. You'll need:

Heavy string

Sturdy darning needles

Thimbles (for kids old enough to use darning needles)

Stale popcorn

Unshelled peanuts

Cranberries

$\frac{1}{2}$ cup peanut butter

2 cups cornmeal or rolled oats

Pine cones

Birdseed

Yarn

Seed bells (available in nurseries or hardware stores)

A suitable bush or tree

QUICK 🖱 PAINLESS

Backyard snow can serve as a giant canvas for a young artist. Give your child some spray bottles set to mist and filled with colored water. She can have a blast painting big pictures in the snow. If she's feeling ready for summer, have her try a beach scene.

1. Let older children string garlands of stale popcorn, peanuts, and cranberries. (Be sure to use stale popcorn because fresh kernels tend to break.)

2. As a safety precaution, have each child wear a thimble to avoid pricked fingers—make sure you supervise! If your kids are too small to work with needles, either string the garlands yourself or skip this step.

3. Stir $\frac{1}{2}$ cup peanut butter into 2 cups of cornmeal or rolled oats.

4. Let your kids spread the peanut-butter mixture onto the pine cones and then roll them in birdseed.

5. Tie some yarn to the top of each pine cone.

6. Have your kids decorate an outdoor Christmas tree or bush with the garlands, pine cones, and seed bells.

7. If desired, your kids also could string smaller garlands to drape as edible necklaces on a snow mom.

Snow Flakes

Children are always fascinated to learn that no two snowflakes are alike. (Actually, we find it pretty amazing, too, but we've never found the time to check enough snowflakes to prove that there isn't a duplicate hiding in there somewhere.)

To help your kids discover the wonder of snowflakes, you'll need:

A sheet of black construction paper, chilled

A magnifying glass

IF YOU'RE SO
INCLINED

If you want to make a permanent record of a snowflake, spray a sheet of chilled glass with chilled hair spray and then help your kids catch several snowflakes on the glass. Allow the crystals to melt at room temperature. They will leave enduring "flake prints" in the hair spray.

1. On a snowy day, send your children outside to catch some snowflakes on a chilled sheet of black construction paper.

2. Let your young scientists examine each crystal through a magnifying glass. Many of the snowflakes will be broken, but they should be able to find a few perfect specimens.

3. Point out the fact that no two flakes are alike!

Snow Ice Cream

Though mugs of hot chocolate are a time-honored tradition on cold winter days, few kids can resist the chance to make and eat this polar treat. For snow ice cream, you'll need:

4 cups fresh, loosely packed snow

A mixing bowl

A large spoon

2 cups milk (or 1 cup of heavy cream)

2 tablespoons vanilla extract

½ cup sugar (or more if the kids are reading this)

Individual serving dishes

Hungry kids

1. Have your kids collect clean, loose snow.

2. Dump 2 quarts of it into a mixing bowl.

3. Sprinkle in the sugar and add the vanilla.

A COMPLETE WASTE OF TIME

The 3 Worst Things to Do on a Snowy Day Are:

1. Bundle up the kids in layer after layer of clothes without first asking if anyone has to go to the bathroom. Someone will.

2. Let the kids "paint" the back steps with their colored spray bottles. One false step and you'll be making snow angels on a hospital bed.

3. Allow the kids to eat maple-syrup pretzels in the nice, warm house. Crunchy turns to gooey and gooey to runny, all before you've got time to say, "Watch ou..."

When you wake up to find fresh snow blanketing the ground, head outside with your children to follow animal tracks. A field guide to animal tracks can help identify what you've found, or you can just have some ridiculous fun letting the kids make up their own stories and names to explain the tracks.

4. Slowly drizzle the milk over the mixture until it gets nice and slushy. Depending on how "wet" the snow was to begin with, you might not need all the milk called for.

5. Serve plain or with a glop of maple or chocolate syrup and then eat!

Snow Pretzels

Give your kids some maple syrup and let them squiggle hand-size figure-eights in a clean patch of snow. The syrup will freeze solid, making a crunchy candy pretzel. What an easy snow recipe!

Getting Time on Your Side

	The Old Way	The Lazy Way
Number of times the kids ask, "Why did it have to rain today?"	3 per hour	0
Number of times you ask, "Why did it have to rain today?"	3.5 per hour	0
Your personal list of things to hate about rain	8 things	Nothing
Snowbound squabbles and squawks	12	3
Number of cartoons the kids watch (and you hear)	11	1
Aspirins per inch of snow	1	0

The Quick and Easy Backyard Gym

With just a few simple tricks, we'll show you how to put together a backyard gym that will give your kids hours of fun and give you hours of laziness.

We also should mention two other important benefits: physical health for the kids and mental health for the parents. Why, that begins to sound tax deductible!

THE FIREBALL FIGHT

Few games have caused more frenzied excitement in our backyard than this one, which our son invented. The game is basically a summer snowball fight with paper wads. You'll need:

Enough kids (or spry adults) to make two teams

Markers

Paper

Two baskets or plastic buckets

Four sheets of orange construction paper

Tape

1. Divide the kids into teams and have each team color sheets of paper (about five per kid) with orange and yellow markers and color one sheet per team with red. Hastily scribbled scrawls of color are fine—there's no need to cover the whole sheet.

2. Show each team how to wad the paper into "fireballs," with the colored side facing out. Completed fireballs go into the team's bucket.

3. Before play begins, tape four sheets of orange construction paper together to make a "lava pit" and place it anywhere in the yard.

4. Set each team loose outdoors armed with their bucket of fireballs and let the battle begin! It's a free-for-all with excited kids running up and down the yard hurling blazing balls at each other.

5. The only rule is that, when a player is hit with one of the rare red balls, he must stand in the lava pit until he counts to 20. (It's more thrilling if he yelps, "Yeowww! I'm burning up in the lava!")

6. There are no winners or losers in a fireball fight—except you. You've gotten your crew to burn off a lot of otherwise pesky energy while they were busy having wild fun.

YOU'LL THANK YOURSELF LATER

Can't scrape together a crowd for a fireball fight? Just two kids will do—or one child and a willing parent. (Aw, go ahead and try it. You'll be surprised by how much fun you have.)

STEP RIGHT UP

The ball-toss booth at the fair usually is a favorite with kids. Here's *The Lazy Way* to set one up in your own backyard. It just takes a few simple supplies. You'll need:

Medium cardboard boxes or

Deep buckets and wastebaskets

Bean bags

1. Arrange the boxes, buckets, and/or wastebaskets in a row.

2. With your child standing back an appropriate distance (this varies with age), have her toss the bean bags into the containers. To add to the fun, call out the score like a carnival barker.

3. After a few pitches, you can turn the barker duties over to a kid and return to paying the bills. Oh, you'd rather stay and play? In that case…

4. Encourage her to practice for as long as she likes.

BOUNCE AND CATCH

Looking for another easy ball game? Here's one that will keep your kids running. You'll need:

A suitable driveway or concrete play area

A plastic cup

A tennis or Ping-Pong ball

IF YOU'RE SO INCLINED

To add challenge to the bean-bag toss, set out some empty coffee cans or even smaller containers. You also might use tennis balls to introduce some extra excitement from the bounce factor. The smaller the container, the higher the score.

1. Show your child how to toss the ball in the air, let it bounce, and then catch the ball in the cup while it's still on its way back up from the ground.

2. Now give her the cup and ball.

3. Encourage her to challenge herself with high—or wild—tosses, the sort that will keep her running all over the place.

MILK JUG CATCH

Here's a great way for your small child to develop catching skills, even when there's no one around to toss him a ball. You'll need:

A large flat wall

An empty milk jug

Scissors

A tennis ball

1. Cut off the top and about halfway down on three sides of a clean, plastic milk jug. Leave the handle so the jug forms an open scoop.

2. Find an appropriate wall outside. (Any wall not facing the street will do, but watch for windows!)

3. Show your child how to toss a tennis ball against the wall and catch it in the jug as it bounces back.

4. Let him keep score. How many catches did he make? (100! 200! 300! Awww, we have to quit—it's dinner time!)

HOMEMADE OBSTACLE COURSE

Picture the Marines in training, scaling tall rope ladders, vaulting over mounds of sand bags, and rounding off the day with a 20-mile run. ("Sir! We are not tired! Sir!") Not to worry. We aren't suggesting anything quite that challenging. In fact, our backyard obstacle course is just plain fun. Here are some suggestions for setting one up. You'll need:

A pad of paper

Boxes, a pile of leaves, or other "found" obstacles

A stopwatch (optional)

1. Size up your yard for its natural attributes—such as porch steps to run up and down, monkey grass to leap over, or a climbing rope to conquer—and make a list of possibilities.

2. Discuss with your kids what should be in the course, jotting down ideas as you go. In addition to your yard's natural attributes, it's fun to work in such treasures as a large cardboard appliance box for kids to crawl through, a double row of medium boxes for them to high step into, or a pile of leaves they must jump over (or into!).

3. Be sure to include some exercise commands, such as "Do five jumping jacks and then hop on one foot down the driveway."

4. When mapping out the course, strive for variety and fun. You might say "Swing across the monkey bars,

As your child's skill improves with the milk jug, reward his persistence by letting him graduate from the jug to a catcher's glove or a handball mitt.

The Lazy Way

stop and make some monkey sounds, and then run around the house two times."

5. The great thing about a backyard obstacle course is that you can change it as often as necessary.

THE SCHWARZENEGGER CAMP

Some kids really respond to an exercise routine that promises to make them stronger. The trick is to create a chart on which they can record their daily progress. Call it the Schwarzenegger Camp and interest will soar. You'll need:

A sheet of paper for each child

A pen

A stopwatch

1. Draw a chart for each child with headings across the top that show the days of the week.

2. Along the side of the chart, fill in the names of exercises such as sit-ups, push-ups, jumping jacks, running in place, and so on.

3. Head outside with your kids and call out exercise orders in your best Austrian accent: "You vill do 10 sit-ups," "You vill run in place for vun minute," and so on.

4. Record the numbers achieved for that day (such as 10 sit-ups, 15 jumping jacks, and so on).

5. In the days that follow, slowly increase the workload and record it on each chart.

You might want to keep the same obstacle course for several months so your kids can clock themselves with a stopwatch and see their speed improve. You'll find that watching them run by is a great way to tone up your neck muscles.

6. It isn't necessary for you to always call out the commands, but it does add to the fun. By the way, there's no law that says parents can't do these exercises along with the kids… well, maybe nature's law—the one that says gravity gets stronger with every passing year.

CRAZY RELAY

A great way to entertain a group of kids—and leave 'em laughing—is to set up a crazy relay. You'll need:

Two paper grocery bags

Two sets of fake noses with glasses

Two big shirts

Two pairs of gloves

Two scarves

Two hats or caps

Two paper plates

1. Fill each grocery bag with a set of the items you've gathered (one shirt, one scarf, and so on).

2. Set the grocery bags on the starting line about four feet apart.

3. Mark the finish line with two paper plates also spaced about four feet apart.

4. Divide the kids into two teams.

5. Explain that the object of the game is for the first person in line to put on all the clothing in the bag (including the nose) and dash to the finish line and back.

Proud of your kids for all that exercise? Why not take them out for a muscle-building fruit shake?

The Lazy Way

6. On his return, the runner must hastily remove the cap, shirt, gloves, scarf, and nose while the next person in line puts them on as fast as he can and repeats the process. (Other team members can help with the mad scramble to dress and undress.)

7. The team that completes the relay first wins.

PASS THE PIGGY

In the heat of summer, a Pass the Piggy relay can't be beat. Just round up the neighborhood kids and get ready for unbridled squeals of excitement. You'll need:

Four large tubs or other containers
Four chairs or stools
A bottle of baby shampoo
A garden hose
A supply of large pink balloons

1. Make two relay lines, marking each start and finish with a tub set on a chair.

2. Add generous squirts of baby shampoo to each tub and fill them up with water from the garden hose.

3. Fill a supply of large pink balloons with water. (Just fit the neck of the balloon over the hose nozzle and turn the water on. If you overfill, you'll probably get squirted a bit as you tie a knot in the neck.)

4. Divide the balloons equally between the two starting-line tubs. Slosh them in the soapy water so they get good and slippery.

QUICK ⬥ PAINLESS

Your backyard will be littered with pink balloon bits after the kids have finished playing Pass the Piggy. To encourage a fast cleanup, offer a prize to the child who collects the most scraps.

5. Divide the kids into two teams and have the teams form a fire brigade line between their start and finish lines.

7. When you say "Go!" the kids must toss their slippery piggies man-to-man down the line as fast as possible.

8. The child at the end must put the piggies into his team's tub at the finish line.

9. After all the piggies in each tub have been tossed in one direction (some will inevitably wriggle loose and go splat), the teams then can pass the remaining piggies in the reverse direction, restoring them to the starting tub.

10. The team that finishes with the most piggies wins.

11. Surviving piggies can be used in a water balloon fight, or you can prolong the fun by having the kids form a circle and toss quivering piggies around and around until the last one breaks.

TUG-OF-WATER

An old-fashioned game of tug-of-war can become even more exciting if you raise the stakes by putting a wading pool in the center. On a hot summer day, the thought of that cool pool can tempt winners to become losers. You'll need:

A small wading pool

A garden hose

A long, thick rope with knots

A COMPLETE WASTE OF TIME

The 3 Worst Things to Do When Playing Pass the Piggy Are:

1. Set up the course on a patch of bare earth. (You'll find out why pigs grunt—so they can find each other in the mud.)

2. Let the kids start playing with the water balloons while you're still trying to fill them up.

3. Put siblings on the same team, unless you enjoy refereeing water-balloon fights.

Have the kids change into their swimsuits before they start playing tug-of-war over a pool. This will save you from having to deal with dripping-wet clothes.

1. Set the wading pool in an open spot in the yard and fill it with water.

2. Divide the kids into teams stationed on opposite sides of the pool.

3. Give the teams the rope and signal to start of the tug-of-war.

4. Both teams will soon wind up in the pool, although the one that went in first is said to have lost the game.

Get Time on Your Side

	The Old Way	The Lazy Way
Worry over kids' lack of exercise	20 minutes per week	0 minutes
Thinking of ways to get the kids to play outside	40 minutes per week	0 minutes
Time for wet floors to dry before the kids are back inside again	10 minutes	40 minutes
Priceless photos you own of the kids in goofy Groucho Marx outfits	0	5
Interruptions by quarreling kids	3 per week	1 per week
Bedtime refrains of "But I'm not tired!"	7 per week	0 minutes

Box City (and Other Boxy Things)

There the kids are outside, whooping and laughing, only three minutes after you set out the most wonderful toy ever invented... and it didn't cost you a penny. Now, that's what we call *The Lazy Way*.

Toy companies have yet to invent a better all-around toy than the basic cardboard box. Almost every parent has seen their child play with a box while the toy it held lay forgotten in the Christmas wrappings. Depending on the box's size, a child can create anything from a wobbly boat to a spaceship control room. Imagine what he'll do with a bunch of boxes!

THE BIG BOX BONANZA

We discovered the fun of large boxes last spring when one of our neighbors set a big stack of them on the curb. We quickly hauled them home—all 12 of them—and stood them in the backyard for our son and his friends to find. When they rounded the corner and saw that fantastic bonanza, they acted as if it was Christmas.

Both appliance stores
and interior decorators
are good sources for
large boxes. Check in
now and then (or leave
your name and number),
and many will let you
know when a bounty is
available.

Give your kids some boxes and a few supplies, and they'll dive into some big projects with only a little help from you. Here are a few suggestions to get them started.

Space Tunnels

Line a row of large boxes end to end—with a few side rooms—and your kids will pretend they're living in alien space tunnels, crewing a submarine, mining deep below the earth, and so on. There's no end to the possibilities! After the project is constructed, your kids will play inside it for days: launching spaceships, venturing out to explore unmapped terrain, and battening down the hatches during fierce wind storms. You'll need:

Large cardboard boxes

A box knife (for adult use only)

Packing tape

Markers

Stickers (optional)

Blankets and pillows (optional)

1. Because large boxes are heavy and bulky, the kids will need your help to arrange them. Before setting a box in place for the tunnel, open the bottom and top flaps. Use a box knife to cut through the tape if necessary.

2. Line up most of the boxes lengthwise with the flaps of each box slipped inside the next to create a long tunnel. At each joint, one upper flap will hang down inside as an invitation for artwork, or it can be

taped to the ceiling by your "tunnel engineers." Reserve two or three boxes for side rooms.

3. To make a side room, cut a door in the wall of a "tunnel" box, lay a second box on its side, position its open end over the doorway, and slide its bottom flap beneath the tunnel. Tape at least the top flap of the room to the tunnel. Follow your child's suggestions about where rooms are needed.

4. Cut windows or hatches at intervals if your kids want them. Most actually prefer mole-like tunnels at first and only later want to add hatches.

5. Turn one box into a command center. Cut a child-level screen into the box's wall and have your kids draw knobs, display screens, and lots of colored buttons to push.

6. Your work is done! From here, your kids can decorate on their own. Our son happened to have some NASA stickers that fit right in. He and his friends also scrawled labels for rooms: Space Lab, Mission Control, and so on.

Variations on a Theme

Large boxes arranged into a tunnel system also can be used as a neighborhood clubhouse. Follow the preceding directions, but leave out the control room (unless your kids want one). Children also might want to pretend the tunnels are rabbit burrows, a secret passage to another world, or a network of sewers patrolled by Ninja Turtles.

IF YOU'RE SO
INCLINED

You can add to box-arranging fun by providing each child with a paint brush and some bright poster paints. Use paper plates as palettes and squirt a different color on each one. Your kids then can personalize their boxes with hand-lettered signs and designs.

Box City

If you stand big boxes upright, they present a whole new opportunity for play. To make a Box City, you'll need:

Large cardboard boxes

A box knife (for adult use only)

Markers

Accessories such as potted plants (optional)

1. Fold the box tops and bottoms shut and stand the boxes upright.

2. Help your kids arrange them as a connected row of buildings or as houses spaced along a street.

3. Cut a door into the back of each box. Also cut a front window at eye level.

4. If the boxes are arranged as a row of buildings, your kids might want you to cut an opening in the side wall of each box so they can crawl from one box to the next.

5. Let your young architects embellish the front of their structures with markers. They might draw hundreds of small windows on a skyscraper, for example, or add shutters and a front door to a home.

Other Boxy Things

A single appliance box can undergo countless transformations with the help of a box knife, some markers, and possibly some toothpaste caps, bottle tops, and glue.

(You'll do all the cutting, of course.) Here are some ideas:

- A television set just the right size to hold a young weather forecaster for a live show
- A time machine (or Dr. Who's Tardis)
- A ticket booth for a backyard circus
- A deluxe roadside lemonade stand
- A puppet stage
- A fortune teller's booth
- A "Members Only" fort
- A duplicating machine (à la Calvin and Hobbes)
- When set lengthwise, a comfortable hideaway (especially if lined with a blanket and pillow)

BOX LOADS OF FUN

Medium-size cardboard boxes present a new range of possibilities for play. Set some out for your young ones; you'll be surprised by the many uses they find for them.

Underwater Subs and Other Contraptions

Two medium-size boxes set back-to-back in a dark room can make a great submarine. First move any dangerous items out of the way. Then give each child a flashlight to probe the surrounding murk for enemy ships. After the sub heads back to port, the same boxes can be used for:

- An airplane with a cockpit and passenger seats. (Or you can arrange two boxes next to each other so a pilot and copilot can guide the plane.)
- Individual space pods for journeys into the unknown.

YOU'LL THANK YOURSELF LATER

Save toothpaste caps and bottle tops for your kids to glue to their boxes. They're great for television knobs, mission-control buttons, and the top-secret controls on a duplicating machine.

- Rubber rafts that must brave Class IV rapids (or a wild slide down the nearest steep, grassy slope).

- Imaginary canoes with sticks for oars. Your kids can pretend to be Lewis and Clark paddling off to explore the West or brave adventurers traveling down the Amazon. ("I say, old chap, is this a monkey's tail or a vine? Oh, not to worry, it's just a snake.")

- For toddlers, four or five cardboard boxes set in a line make a wonderful train.

Squirrel Traps

Every so often, our son decides he's going to catch a squirrel for a pet. He never succeeds, but he always manages to prove that the real joy of the hunt lies in the planning. He spends hours absorbed with his plotting, often drawing dozens of variations on his traps.

To make a squirrel trap, you'll need:

A medium cardboard box

A box knife (for adult use only)

A length of string

Masking tape

Some nuts

Snacks (for the kids not the furry mammals)

1. Cut the top flaps off the box and seal the bottom flaps.

2. Poke a small hole in the center of the bottom of the box.

3. Thread string through the hole and tie it in a big knot on the inside.

4. Tape the knot to the box with masking tape.

5. Get some snacks ready for the kids to take with them.

6. Have your kids place the nuts in a little pile under a nice, climbable tree. They then can climb the tree and wait for an unsuspecting squirrel to come along. Boom! They lower the box and they've got their squirrel.

7. You love peace and quiet; the kids love the thrill of the stakeout. When it doesn't work (and it won't), the blame falls on that crafty squirrel.

SMALL STUFF

Shoe boxes, pizza boxes, and even fast-food soft-drink holders can be turned into toys by an imaginative child. As with large and medium boxes, few supplies are necessary.

Mardi Gras Floats

School children in southern Louisiana make miniature Mardi Gras floats every Carnival season. Your kids can try this, too, or they might prefer to make a float based on another event they know, such as the Macy's Thanksgiving Day Parade or the Rose Bowl Parade. You'll need:

A shoe box (without top) for each child

Colored tissue paper (for Mardi Gras, use purple, green, and gold)

YOU'LL THANK YOURSELF LATER

Caution your squirrel hunters not to handle their quarry should they succeed (a virtual impossibility—but don't tell them that!). Perhaps somewhere there exists a really stupid squirrel that won't hear them whispering or munching cookies and that can't smell human all over a suspicious box.

Your kids can build a two-tiered float by taping a small box to the top of their shoe-box creation and then covering it with tissue paper.

Scissors

Tape

String

Colored straws

Colored feathers

School glue

Decorations such as sequins, beads, or small plastic dolls or soldiers to ride on the floats

1. Have your kids wrap the outside of their shoe box with colored tissue paper and tape.

2. Now it's your turn. Using the point of the scissors, drill a small hole in the front of the shoe box and thread three or four feet of string through it.

3. Let your kids knot the string on the inside of the shoe box and tape it securely. (The string will be the float's pull.)

4. Now your turn again. Turn the shoe box upside down. Using scissors, drill two holes in the new "top." Let your kids stick straws in the holes.

5. Have your kids stuff colorful feathers into the top of each straw until they look like multihued palm trees. Glue them in place if necessary.

6. For a final touch, let the kids embellish their floats with the decorative items you provide.

7. After the floats are finished, your kids can parade them up and down the driveway and along the sidewalk using the string pulls.

You Want Pepperoni with That?

Did you know that your pizza guy delivers more than just good stuff to eat? As it turns out, the box can be fun to play with, too.

To prepare, eat the pizza (we needed to tell you that?), remove any sticky stuff, air the box out overnight, and it's ready to use.

Here are some suggestions for what a pizza box can become:

■ It's a shield! Cut two half-moons in the back of the box, leaving a cardboard strip between them to use as a handle. Have your kids draw fierce decorations on the front with markers.

■ It's a high-tech briefcase! Your kids can write "Top Secret" on the outside and draw their own set of spy tools on the inside. They also can create an array of launch buttons… anything they think a spy should have!

■ It's a game! Cut a ½-inch diameter hole in the bottom, place two different-colored marbles inside at opposite corners, close the lid, and have the kids try to roll out just the right color.

Behold! The Lowly Holder

Take a new look at the paper soft-drink holders used by many fast-food places. These humble mounds of molded pulp can easily be transformed into mountains, villages, or rocky landscapes in which to play with small toys. Just turn them upside down and let your kids paint them. Play can begin as soon as the holders are dry.

IF YOU'RE SO
INCLINED

Pizza-box shields come in very handy during the fast and furious fireball fights described in Chapter 8.

Getting Time on Your Side

	The Old Way	The Lazy Way
Time needed to build a backyard fort	12 hours	10 minutes
Time needed to turn the backyard fort into tunnels, a city, or a space ship	Huh?	10 minutes
Cost to provide a backyard fort	$250	$0
Time needed to convince the kids to picnic in a tree for an hour and a half	2 hours	15 minutes
Find your kids a new toy	40 minutes	2 minutes
Go to Mardi Gras	7 days	30 minutes

Chapter

ten

Raking Up the Lazy Way

Yard work is the bane of childhood, but not to children of *Lazy Way* parents. To them, it's all fun and games, and no one even has to mention "allowance" or "duty" or has to yell "because it's your job!"

True, grim-faced laborers probably could accomplish these tasks in a tenth of the time required by a gaggle of giggling kids, but at what cost to the soul?

AUTUMN CELEBRATION

When the weather turns crisp and the leaves have fluttered into crunchy drifts in the yard, the whole family can enjoy a little camaraderie by raking up together. Call your work day an Autumn Celebration and little hands will barely notice they're doing chores. For that matter, neither will you.

Here's our lazy recipe for complete success. You'll need:

A card or picnic table

A generous supply of snacks

A rake for each helper

A box of lawn bags

1. Have your kids invite some friends over for your Autumn Celebration.

2. Set out a table piled high with snacks—cider and doughnuts, muffins, apple slices and grapes, and gooey Halloween cupcakes.

3. Give everyone a rake and set out your box of lawn bags.

4. Let the games begin! The following sections provide some great ideas.

Leaf Mazes

It never hurts to start with a little confusion. If your yard is large enough, divide your crew into teams and let them challenge each other by making leaf mazes. This gives you a head start on the raking without having to worry about the diligence of your helpers. (Hint: A good place to hide a dead end is around a corner or behind a bush.)

After both teams have conquered the mazes, your kids can make minor alterations to change the paths into big leaf roadways. These are good for quick, adrenaline-charged sprints around the yard before returning to the work at hand. (Work? How silly. We meant to say play!)

Obstacle Courses

Piles of leaves can be put to good use in an outdoor obstacle course. Join your kids in converting the road-ways made earlier into mounds of leaves throughout the yard. Here are some suggestions for obstacle-course fun:

■ Make some small piles of leaves for kids to jump over.

- Make some big piles of leaves for kids to jump into.

- Arrange the piles throughout the yard so the contestants must dash from one to the next.

- Convert a few straight pathways into squiggly ones so the kids must navigate between leaf piles.

- For extra fun, have your Olympians start the course wearing shoe boxes on their feet. They must shuffle from the starting line to the first pile of leaves, jump out of the boxes, and then continue on to the next challenge.

- Include a stretch in which everyone must hop or crawl.

- Add to the excitement by placing an enormous pile of leaves at the very end. (This is a jump-in pile, of course.)

Snack Break

Pace the fun and games by making time for periodic snack breaks to reinforce the notion that this is an Autumn Celebration and not a work day. Besides, once you're an adult, you don't get many excuses to gobble down several cupcakes in a row. On this one day, let *carpe diem* (seize the day) become *carpe* cupcake!

Bagging the Question

Which team can bag the most leaves? Will it be the Bagatelles, the Bagpipers of Bagdad, the Bag Men, or the Bilbo Baggins Baggers? After all the leaves have been raked into huge mounds, bagging can commence. Form

IF YOU'RE SO INCLINED

To add a competitive edge to your obstacle-course fun, use a stopwatch to time the contestants— then give it a go yourself.

teams and assign them to leaf piles of equal size (unless the Big Bag Boys team needs to be handicapped with a larger pile). Even though it's always sad to lose a leaf pile, the fun of these contests will divert attention from the sacrifice.

- Which team can stuff and tie a bag the fastest?
- Which team can bag all its leaves first?
- Which team can relay a bag to the end of the line (at the curb) in the shortest amount of time?
- Which team can make up the craziest leaf-bagging song?

Treasure Hunt

Another way to work a little fun into bagging leaves is to hide a half-sheet of yellow construction paper under one of the piles. The rules state that, once a kid starts on a pile, it must be completely bagged before she can move on to another pile. When someone finds the sheet, award her 10 points and then hide the sheet again. The child with the most points when all the work is done is declared the winner.

A variation of this works well when you're raking with just your own family. Plant a series of clues under the piles. You might begin, for example, with a message under the first pile stating "Search in the pile to your right" or "Walk 10 steps forward and search there." Every pile your kids encounter must be raked, of course. (Let them search for clues as a team rather than in competition—didn't Cain whack Abel with a rake for stealing his clue?)

Along with the clues, you might want to include coupons for various treats—some funny, some special. Here are a few ideas:

- Congratulations! You've won some licks from the dog!

- This coupon lets you invite a friend over.

- Cash this in for a high-five from Dad.

- Good going! You've earned a trip to the park tomorrow.

- Thanks for your hard work. Head inside for home-made brownies and a hug from Mom. (A special coupon hidden under the last pile.)

SPRING AND SUMMER

Outside chores during spring and summer range from planting vegetables and flowers to mulching, watering, cleaning up, and pulling weeds. (Older kids also can mow the grass.) Most children enjoy digging in the dirt at planting time, but they often are less enthusiastic about other garden duties. Here are some ideas for putting some zest into regular old yard work.

Weeding

Can your children tell the difference between your zinnias and parsley and an upstart weed? If you're not sure, spend some time showing them what to look for and how to weed properly (it's important to get roots and all) and then challenge everyone to a weed-pulling contest. Some suggested winning categories are:

IF YOU'RE SO INCLINED

Before your weed competition begins, explain that you'll subtract 20 points (er, weeds) for each mistake a child makes in pulling up a vegetable or a flower. (With luck, this stringent penalty will help make sure there are no mis-tackes.)

- The biggest weed
- The smallest weed
- The weirdest weed
- The most weeds of one kind
- The most weeds altogether

Job Tag

If your list of yard chores is long enough to keep the whole family busy for at least an hour, why not write each task on a slip of paper and drop it into a job jar? If some chores are suitable for adults only (such as pruning), put those in a separate container. Try to make each task only 15 minutes long. Write "Weed the front section of the bed by the driveway," for example, instead of assigning the whole bed. You'll need:

A job jar with tasks for kids

A job jar with tasks for adults (if applicable)

The necessary yard tools

1. Herd everyone outside and announce that you'll be playing Job Tag.

2. Explain the rules: Mom or Dad is "it." When a person is tagged, he must draw a task from the job jar. (The non-"it" parent is fair game as well.)

3. After everyone has been caught, "it" must draw a task as well.

4. To add a few giggles, groan with mock dismay at the task you pull. "Oh, nooo! Not edging! I hate edging!"

5. After the first round of chores is finished, play again. This time start with a different person being "it."

Help Wanted

It never hurts to advertise when you want a job done. Most kids like to earn extra moolah by doing extra chores. If your family has a bulletin board in the kitchen or in another central area, use index cards to let your kids know what jobs are available and—even more important—how much each one pays. (If the price is right, you might even want to take some on yourself.)

At the Car Wash

On a hot summer day, let your kids wear their bathing suits to wash the car—they probably won't consider it a job. Be prepared, however. After the car has been lathered and the last kid has taken his turn rinsing with the hose, attention will drift to the wild excitement of squirting each other and playing in the water. But that's okay. The job is already done.

The Younger Set

Small children might not be much help with outdoor work, but they like to tag along and do what they can. Some garden centers sell child-size rakes, shovels, and hoes to keep little hands busy. You also can find small wheelbarrows, plastic toy lawnmowers, and other yard equipment to make little ones feel like they're "big guys." The most important part is to try to think of ways to include them in your work. They can:

YOU'LL THANK YOURSELF LATER

Keep a sprinkler handy when your kids wear their bathing suits to wash the car. That way, they can whoop and run through the water when their work is done.

- Help put leaves in lawn bags (with frequent breaks to jump in the big piles).

- Drag a lawn bag to the curb, with a little assistance from you.

- Gently place mulch around plants.

- Water plants with a small watering can.

- Help harvest vegetables or pick berries (and eat a few).

- Pick up and stack branches you've pruned with hand clippers.

- Busy themselves with gathering acorns.

- If you hang clothes in the yard, they can hang up wash cloths, doll clothes, and other small items on their own kid-size clothesline.

Getting Time on Your Side

	The Old Way	The Lazy Way
Making your kids do chores	20 minutes	5 minutes
Settling fights over whose turn it is to...	10 minutes per day	0 minutes
Helpers visible when seeking volunteers for yard work	0	All of 'em
Handling kid problems while supposedly weeding	20 minutes	0 minutes
Getting the car washed	20 minutes	5 minutes
Dreading your announcement that it's time to clean the yard	5 days	0 minutes

Indoors for Some Quick Innings

Are You Too Lazy to Read "Indoors for Some Quick Innings?"

1 You plan to start reading right after breakfast, which you hope to eat while the kids take their afternoon nap. ☐ Yes ☐ No

2 You're saving it to read in that golden month between the last kid leaving for college and the arrival of the first grandchild. ☐ Yes ☐ No

3 Your kids are inside today, and they're using the book as home plate. ☐ Yes ☐ No

Weather Days: 10 Quick Tips for Survival

Too dark, too wet, too hot, or too cold to play outside? Here are the best of the best no-sweat ideas that really work!

Of course, if the situation already is bad and the cries of cooped up kids are drowning even the roar of thunder and the rumble of rain rushing down the waterspouts, you might need to apply several of these terrific tips in succession before everything is back under control. That's why we call them tips instead of miracles.

Rush off now for a quick skim through the chapter before your nervous system collapses. You can return later for a more leisurely, *Lazy Way* read after you've got the little folks safely settled down, you poor dear.

TIP #1. TURN WALL-BOUNCING INTO EXERCISE

Kids and clouds have a lot in common on a rainy day: They're both full of lightning. The best way to discharge that pent-up energy is to work it off, and here are some of our favorite tricks to get that job done.

You're in the Army Now

When your troop's energy levels are so high that only exercise will save the day, transform yourself into a friendly army sergeant and order a drill. You'll need:

A whistle (optional)

A chinning bar

1. In your best army voice, call your recruits to attention. (Or, even better, blow a whistle and say "Atten-HUT!")

2. After you've established command, order your troops to do a fixed number of sit-ups and push-ups followed by a round of jumping jacks. ("Yes, Sir!")

3. Next, propel your kids down the hall on their hands in wheelbarrow fashion and have them finish up at the chinning bar.

4. If one child is old enough to assume command, you can give her a field promotion to corporal. That way, the drills can continue should the first set of exercises not quite discharge all the squirminess in your squad.

YOU'LL THANK YOURSELF LATER

Brush up on Army lingo to make your role as sergeant more convincing. You'll lead your platoon through PT (physical training). At "lights out," each private will bed down in the barracks. They'll rise at reveille, brush their teeth in the latrine, and turn out for inspection.

The Work-Out Continues

Kids still bouncing off the walls? Try these ideas:

- Challenge your children to imitate the movements of various animals. Some suggestions include elephant, snake, bird, kangaroo, sea anemone, dolphin, polar bear, and frog. Have fun and try for some giggles.

- Make a hopscotch grid on the floor with masking tape. (If you've forgotten the rules of hopscotch, check out *Hopscotch, Hangman, Hot Potato, and Ha, Ha, Ha: A Rulebook of Children's Games* by Jack Maquire.)

- Try indoor rock-hopping. Cut rocks out of cardboard and tape them to the floor. Have your kids imagine they're braving a creek crossing made of slippery rocks.

IF YOU'RE SO INCLINED

For a variation on indoor rock-hopping, let your kids pretend that—yikes!—they're trying to make their way through a deadly lava flow.

TIP #2. LET 'EM ROLL THEIR OWN

Many of our favorite ways to roll away boredom begin by rolling out a newspaper end roll (see Chapter 1 for details). It's the busy parent's Old Faithful. An eye-popping expanse of blank paper is an invitation to fun that few kids can resist. You'll need:

A newspaper end roll (a roll of butcher paper also works)

Masking tape

Washable markers or crayons

Scissors

A stapler

IF YOU'RE SO
INCLINED

Newspaper end rolls also are great for making banners. Your kids might want to make signs that cheer on a favorite team, that celebrate a birthday, or that welcome a visiting friend.

Indoor Mural

1. Create a blank mural space by taping a generous length of newspaper end roll to the floor.

2. If your kids can't think of anything to draw, toss out some suggestions: an underwater scene, the rain forest, a summer day in the mountains, a space battle, or a cut-away look at the inside of your home on Christmas Eve. (Are the reindeer pawing on the roof? Is that Santa munching cookies? Is everyone asleep?)

3. After the mural is finished, help your kids tape it to a wall.

Life-Size Paper Dolls

1. With your child lying on the paper, trace around her to form an outline.

2. Let her cut out the silhouette and color in the figure however she likes. She might draw herself in her favorite clothes or might turn herself into an explorer, an astronaut, a princess, or a cowgirl.

3. Tape the resulting self-portrait to the door of her room.

Paper People

1. Loosely trace your child's outline on the paper, allowing an extra inch all around.

2. Using this first outline as a template, trace nine more copies.

3. Cut out all the silhouettes and group them in pairs.

4. Starting at the feet, begin stapling the edges of each pair together. As you go, stuff the insides with crumpled newspaper to make life-size figures.

5. From here, the possibilities can be as elaborate as your child likes. She can attach long strips to make hair, cut out paper patterns and make clothes, or—as our son, potentially a future doctor, did—cut out patterns for the liver, heart, lungs, and gizzard to make them anatomically authentic.

Paper people make great friends, mostly because they are such good listeners. We've found that they like sitting in chairs where they have a view out the window, and they apparently enjoy cookies, which always disappear when they're around. We've never actually seen them eat one, but our son has. Whatever you do, however, don't serve milk to paper people because they make a soggy mess of themselves when attempting to drink it.

Monumental Map

Using a big sheet of paper so everyone can help with the drawing, have your kids create an oversized map of the neighborhood. The map can include all their favorite spots: the peaceful forest, Jack's house, the climbing tree, and so on. (The city can include the ice cream shop, the park, Sarah's apartment…)

TIP #3. THREE BOXES OF FUN

Interest in artwork flagging? Pull out the dress-up box, the Little Guys box, or the indoor sandbox (see Chapter 3 for details). You also might want to rotate toys. Some

YOU'LL THANK YOURSELF LATER

When you come across activity pages in the newspaper or comics such as Where's Waldo?, cut them out and save them. They're great for keeping kids busy on bad-weather days.

parents set aside a special set of rainy-day toys that only are made available when the children are trapped inside by bad weather. These are then put away the moment the sun peeks through the clouds.

TIP #4. RAINY-DAY CUTUPS

Here's what you'll need:

Old magazines or catalogs

Scissors

Glue

Large sheets of paper

Lunch-size paper bags

1. Have the kids make some Salvador Dalí-style collages. Lead the way by making one of your own—a weird mix of unlikely elements, the stranger the better—then let them try their hand. Fancy a cow floating above a swimming pool with a city skyline in the background and diamond necklaces raining down? How about a tiny adult sitting in front of a giant bowl of dog food?

2. Have you seen those books that let you mix and match heads and bodies? Let your kids do that with magazine pictures. Demonstrate with one of your own, maybe putting a beautiful model's head on a baby's body or putting a toddler's grinning face on a fluffy cat. Encourage your kids to make wild family or class portraits with these funny forms.

QUICK ⬤ PAINLESS

3. Give each of your kids a paper bag. Ask them to go through magazines and cut out 10 things they like, 10 things they don't like, and 10 things they'd like to become better at, such as swimming or math. Have them put all these into the bag. (Tell them they can cut out words as well as pictures.) When everyone is finished, have the kids take turns pulling out and explaining each item they've placed in their bag.

4. Have your kids flip through magazines and cut out foods they'd like to eat. Then have them spread out their ingredients and brainstorm ways to combine them into meals. This might lead you to discover some new dishes for dinnertime such as our recent favorite—bacon-wrapped hot dogs with a mound of macaroni laced with pimentos and chunks of crunchy celery.

5. Your kids can cut out pictures of famous faces and paste them to the front of their paper bag. Cut eye holes and they can while away a little time pretending to be someone else.

TIP #5. A SCRAPPY IDEA

Bad-weather days can be great for working on projects such as scrapbooks. You'll need:

The scrapbook items you've been saving

School glue

Scissors (the zigzag kind are extra fun)

QUICK ●π● PAINLESS

For instant fun, give each of your kids some old newspapers and a pencil with an eraser. Show them how easy it is to erase parts of a newspaper photo and fill in the blanks with humorous details.

Some kids also can be inspired to start a journal, particularly after seeing a movie such as *Harriet the Spy,* in which the heroine records her thoughts in a marble composition book. A look-alike notebook, placed in little hands at the just right moment, might start a lifelong habit.

Pens

Labels

A blank scrapbook (one per child)

1. Show your kids how to loosely arrange items chronologically (before vacation, after vacation, right about when school started, and so on).

2. Trim the photos and other items to fit if necessary.

3. Glue them into the book.

4. Encourage the kids to write captions as necessary (to identify friends in a photo, for example).

5. When they're finished, be sure to have them show you the results.

TIP #6. COIN MAGIC

When the kids are hopping about like Mexican jumping beans, just get out the big loose-change jar you've been saving since way back in Chapter 3. You'll need:

The loose change jar

Coin wrappers (available from any bank)

1. Dramatically dump all the money into a big heap on the kitchen table as you announce, "Let's see if we've got enough money saved up to go someplace today."

2. Show little kids how to make one dollar stacks of 10 dimes, 4 quarters, and so on.

3. After they've made the stacks, hand out the coin wrappers, have your kids wrap the change in the proper sleeves, and tally the results.

4. With luck, you'll have enough saved for an outing to the movies or at least for ice cream cones.

TIP #7. A PICNIC WITHOUT ANTS

Add a little punch to their lunch by spreading an old tablecloth on the floor and having an indoor picnic.

This simple change from the ordinary can do wonders for flagging spirits. Avoid a mess by using drink cups with lids and straws. (It's a rule of physics that glasses will spill spontaneously when set anywhere on a floor shared with wiggly feet.) After lunch, make a net by slinging the tablecloth or a blanket across two chairs and let the gang play a bang-up round of balloon volleyball. Have extra balloons ready if you have one of those "popcorn-" textured ceilings.

TIP #8. AN INDOOR TREASURE HUNT

Have your kids follow a series of clues to find a prize—a plate of cookies, some wrapped dollar-store items, or a 500-piece puzzle (a clever choice that will keep them busy for hours). Write your clues on small strips of paper and hide them throughout the house. "Look in the fruit bowl," for example, might lead to "Check under Spot's bed."

The longer the paper trail, the more time they'll spend. One way to stretch things out—and to help your

QUICK ⬛ PAINLESS

Need a fast game for two kids? Let them play table hockey with a cotton ball and two straws as hockey sticks. In a quieter version of this game, they can blow puffs of air through the straws to move the cotton ball.

Heavy snow is predicted for three more days? Now might the time to check out a book about magic from the library so your kids can try some simple tricks. If they really get inspired, they could put on a show. (You and the dog can pay admission; the whole show ought to be just long enough to hold the dog's interest.)

crew expend some pent-up energy—is to build some exercise into the clues. For example, "Touch your toes 10 times, crawl to the end of the hall, and look to your left." Some kids have so much fun with treasure hunts that, after the original chase is over, they take turns setting up trails of their own.

If your kids already have done our Spy vs. Spy tip (#9) and know how to develop a secret message, write "Secret Message" on some of the clue sheets and write those clues in invisible ink.

TIP #9. SPY VS. SPY

One rainy-day activity that always amazes kids is writing invisible messages. All you need is:

Lemon juice (or extract)

A paintbrush

Paper

1. Have the kids write a secret message using a paintbrush dipped in lemon juice.

2. After they've written their secret message, have them hold it close to a glowing lamp bulb to watch the letters magically appear. Be careful that little fingers don't touch the hot bulb, of course.

TIP #10. SOUND GAMES

Have you ever thought about how sound-effects artists create the background sounds we hear on the radio, on TV, and at the movies? The crunch of footsteps on gravel, the clip-clop of horses' hooves, the crack of a breaking beam? With the help of a minicassette recorder, your kids can try this out on their own. Part of the secret is to actively listen to the sounds around you and then apply them to different situations.

- Gently crumpling the cellophane wrapper from a box of cough drops can sound like a campfire. Crumple more vigorously to sound like a forest fire.

- The sound of a diving board (and also some really spooky music) can be made by flipping the end of a ruler poked over the edge of a table while dragging it inward.

- Slowly and rhythmically rub the teeth of a comb over a round drawer pull or a table edge to get either the creak of Grandma's rocker or the sound of a chirping cricket with a head cold.

- Most pocket tape recorders have two speeds. Record the air rushing through an air-conditioner vent using the fast speed (2.4 cm) and then play it back using the slow speed (1.2 cm) for the convincing rumble of a stampeding herd of buffalo.

Older kids can play a challenging game of Guess the Sound by taking turns with the tape recorder. They might even record themselves announcing "radio static," for example, followed by what actually is a deck of cards being slowly riffled. The other kids have to guess what actually made the noise they heard. Younger kids will find the game challenging even without false clues.

IF YOU'RE SO
INCLINED

If your kids don't have access to a tape recorder, consider an inexpensive toy version such as the Yak Bak. Kids can experiment with sound by digitally recording short sequences and then playing them back at altered speeds.

Getting Time on Your Side

	The Old Way	The Lazy Way
Time spent getting kids to play	90 minutes	15 minutes
Time spent pulling kids off curtains	10 minutes	0 minutes
Time spent enduring mindless video game music	120 minutes	0 minutes
Number of aspirin per parent	2	0
Times you hear "I'm bored"	15	2
Time spent calming rainy-day quarrels	18 minutes	5 minutes

Tinkering Around

Plastic bottle caps, rubber bands, old parts, and other wonders gathered in a special tinkering place are a powerful magnet to hold children's attention.

Not only that, unstructured messing around is one of the secrets to developing a creative mind. Give kids some junk and a place to fiddle and explore. You'll be amazed (or at least amused) by the inventive results.

THE EDISON EFFECT

We suggested in Chapter 3 that you find a good spot for your kid's puttering place. At times, you'll tinker there together; at times, they'll tinker alone. In every case, however, your kids will have the chance to do some outside-the-box thinking as they escape the predictable conformity of prepackaged toys.

What goes into a tinkering place? Here are some suggestions:

- Age-appropriate tools (pliers, files, small Phillips- and flat-head screwdrivers—the stuff Dad might want to borrow now and then when he's misplaced his own tools)

- Safety goggles

- Broken appliances, such as toasters or blow dryers, with the cords cut off (avoid items with vacuum tubes—TVs especially— anything with chemicals, and clocks with tightly wound mainsprings)

- Household castoffs such as an old computer keyboard or a broken light switch

- Scraps of wood and some nails, screws, and wood glue

- String, lightweight rope, and maybe some old pulleys

- Large rubber bands

- Wire and wire cutters

- Plastic plumbing pipes

- Marbles and Ping-Pong balls

- Springs from various appliances

- A magnifying glass, magnets, and other basic scientific equipment

- Old books with complicated diagrams and drawings that kids can pretend to build

It's also a good idea to include your family's crafts bin (see Chapter 3) in your tinkering place. Many of its supplies go hand-in-hand with puttering, and it's nice to have all the messy stuff confined to one spot. If you prefer to keep your crafts bin elsewhere, consider duplicating key supplies such as school glue, washable paint and markers, and paint brushes.

QUICK ☺ PAINLESS

Have the guys at the hardware store cut your ½-inch plumbing pipe for you. You want one- and two-foot lengths. To make sure the pipes slip easily into the joints, pick up some sheets of 110 sandpaper to polish the cut ends.

The Set-up

It's helpful to provide your kids with good lighting, a small peg board for arranging their tools, and some shelves and bins to store supplies. We've found that adding an old couch or some chairs and even a beat-up rug makes their tinkering place a great place to hang out while they're thinking up projects. (If your pint-size inventors manage to erect a pulley system, you can relay a bag of snacks from the kitchen to the lab.)

Name That Whatchamacallit

Every great puttering place needs a name, and your kids will want to exercise their pride of ownership by naming theirs. Besides, it's huge fun thinking one up, and it provides your kids with their first concrete project—painting the sign.

What To Do

Even within one family, kids will approach a tinkering place in different ways. One child we know spends hours taking apart old appliances to see how they work. (This is called reverse engineering and should look impressive under "Hobbies" on her college application.) Another child fiddles with sticks, string, stones, and rubber bands to make catapults and other shooting contraptions. Yet another child makes artistic arrangements on wood by combining drawings, glued-down coins, and colored wires woven between upright nails. The common denominator is that they all spend hours happily absorbed in their work.

YOU'LL THANK YOURSELF LATER

To help form good work habits, try to include some organization aids in your kids' tinkering spot: a tool rack, peg-board hangers, and lots of small boxes or containers to hold all the tiny screws they'll be taking out of stuff.

Other projects that kids will enjoy in their tinkering spot are:

- Working on rock, feather, leaf, or insect collections
- Conducting simple science experiments
- Fiddling around with magnets, prisms, and the like
- Studying leaves or bugs through a magnifying glass
- Imaginative play such as making a space capsule from an old computer keyboard and a camera tripod or making a (nonworking) robot from a mix of parts such as a headlight and a hubcap
- Trying to make inventions that actually work (though often a little tweaking is needed from Mom or Dad)
- Working on elaborate projects such as building a homemade fort

Fortunately, there is no right or wrong way to putter. That's what makes it fun!

PROJECT *LAZY WAY*

Most kids don't need encouragement when it comes to fooling around. It's grownups who need an excuse to play—that's why some of these projects are so appealing to followers of *The Lazy Way*. Sure, they demonstrate science, but they're also a blast to do.

Fountain of Foam

Here's some real chemical magic with heaps of foam. No matter how many times we do this, we still find it absolutely amazing. Try it as an inaugural activity for your science lab. You and your little chemists will need:

A small bowl

A measuring cup

Tap water

One package unflavored gelatin

A teaspoon (for stirring and measuring)

Three drinking glasses

3 teaspoons baking soda

3 teaspoons alum

A pie plate

1. In a small bowl, mix the package of gelatin with ¼ cup hot water to make a gelatin solution. Little fingers will enjoy poking this gooey mess.

2. To ½ glass of water, stir in the baking soda and 2 teaspoons of the gelatin solution.

3. To a second ½ glass of water, mix in the alum.

4. Place an empty glass in the center of a pie plate (to catch the foam overflow).

5. With a wild look in your eye, announce that you will create some foam. Simultaneously pour the two solutions into the empty glass. (For effect, you can mutter like a mad magician as you pour.)

6. Whoa!!!! Look at all the foam!

7. Good thing you have some leftover gelatin solution. Your kids will want to see that wild mountain of foam erupt again and again.

Hurray! The kid's tinkering place is in business. (Hear the distant tink, tink, tink of happy kids?) This means you've earned a little puttering time of your own. Pull out a favorite project and revel in the lack of interruptions.

The Lazy Way

Snap, Crackle, and... They're Alive!

Another high-charged experiment requires a balloon and a bowl of dry Rice Krispies cereal. Have your kids rub the inflated balloon on their hair until it becomes charged with static electricity (four or five quick rubs is plenty).

Immediately dip the charged balloon into the bowl of Rice Krispies. The static electricity will attract a bunch of rice puffs. Next have one of the kids slowly bring their finger toward the peacefully clinging rice puffs. Suddenly the puffs all scuttle away as if they were alive! Like the foam, kids find the reaction so neat they repeat it time and again.

Paper Cup Telephones

Did you make these telephones when you were young? Even in the age of cell phones, kids find them fascinating. You'll need:

Two paper cups

Thin string or thread

Two match sticks

1. Poke a hole in the bottom of each paper cup.

2. Thread one end of the string through each hole.

3. Knot the ends of the string around the center of the match stick so that the string, when pulled taut, brings the stick into contact with the bottom of the paper cup.

Now the kids can set up their own paper-cup phone line, as long as they're careful to keep the string taut

between the two cups. One kid talks into his cup while the other listens with the second cup to his ear. It works for tree house-to-ground communications and makes a nifty addition to Box City (see Chapter 9).

WATER FIREWORKS

You and your child will be fascinated by water fireworks. You'll see sinuous plumes of color plunging downward, making fantastic nebulae that rotate slowly and then curl off into beautiful filaments. In addition to the fun, however, you'll also see some really interesting science. For water fireworks, you'll need:

Bottles of dark-blue and dark-red food coloring

A see-through bowl or glass

Water

A ruler

1. Fill the bowl with water and let it stand a few minutes until it is calm.

2. Using the ruler as a rough guide, squeeze out a blue droplet from roughly 6½ inches above the water. It will hit the water at just under 4 miles per hour. How deep does the color go?

3. When the water's calm again, squeeze a red droplet from about 1½ inches above the water. This one hits at about 2 miles per hour—only half as fast. Note how far below the surface it goes. Surprised?

4. Now for the big fun. Pick your favorite color and watch the droplet hit the surface from above (from

any height). Wow! You'll see a terrific explosion of colored lines zooming out and then swirling into feathers at the periphery of the impact circle.

Q&A: Why did the slower droplet dive deeper?

The faster a droplet hits, the more its energy is directed into a sideways splat when the water's surface cannot give way quickly enough. A slower impact allows the droplet to stay together so it can punch its way deeper.

Q&A: Why does the droplet make lines?

When the droplet punches in, the surface tension on the water is shattered in the center (just like a plate of glass). Continued tension from the edges yanks the broken surface toward the walls of the glass. This sucks color from the droplet up the "cracks," letting you see them as radial lines. (Soap reduces surface tension. If you add a little soapy water, you'll stop seeing any lines at all.)

Want to see inertia in action?

Now that the bowl is laced with a pattern of fireworks, pick it up gently and let one of the kids hold it in his hands. Make sure you're on a light-colored floor so the fireworks patterns can easily be seen. Have him look down into the bowl as he slowly turns in a circle. The water will seem to be turning in the opposite direction!

(Actually, the water is standing still due to the force of inertia. The bowl is sliding around it.)

Instant Puzzle

Give your kids a mental workout by dropping a nail into a gallon jug. Challenge them to retrieve the nail without picking up the jug or tipping it over. They can use one or all of the following supplies:

- A stick (a foot or so in length)
- A foot or so of flexible wire
- A 5" by 2" strip of aluminum foil
- An unchewed stick of gum
- A rubber band

There are at least five solutions to the problem, so your kids should be able to work one out. If they get stuck, however, give them a tasty hint—they can chew the gum.

IF YOU'RE SO
INCLINED

One clear day, have the kids lay a big sheet of paper outside. After a few hours, lift the edges to collect fallen dust into the center. With a strong magnet held under the pile, gently tip the sheet. The dark, pitted spheres that remain are micrometeorites!

Getting Time on Your Side

	The Old Way	The Lazy Way
Time spent searching for Dad's tools	15 minutes	0 minutes (You know just where to look.)
Time spent convincing your kids that science is fun	Weeks… maybe forever	0 minutes
Time available for your own projects	20 minutes	2 hours
Number of "I'm bored" statements	5 per day	0 minutes
Time spent searching for the kids	15 minutes	0 minutes (They're with Dad's tools.)
Amount of creativity, wackiness, and surprises	Some	Lots

Chapter thirteen

Hassle-Free Crafts

Kids messing with crafts needn't make you cross—not once you've discovered these wily ways to while away the time.

Craft work is an important rite of passage. It develops hand-eye coordination, encourages artistic expression, and promotes chest-thumping pride. (It'll do this for your kids, too.) Moreover, every household needs weird-looking stuff to hang on the walls.

FASHION STATEMENT IN PASTA TENSE

For wardrobe accessories with that simple yet elegant look, have your kids string up a batch of colorful pasta jewelry. Your young craftsmen might choose to make everyday pasta beads in green, blue, and yellow, or they might go for a seasonal look with orange and brown at Halloween or red and green at Christmas. You'll need:

A large bag of dry rigatoni (or any other tube pasta)

One sealable plastic bag for each color

Food coloring

A newspaper

Yarn

Scissors

A pencil

Day One

1. Portion out the dry rigatoni into separate plastic bags.

2. Let your kids squirt a liberal amount of food coloring into each bag.

3. Have them shake the bags to thoroughly coat the pasta. (Oops! Don't forget to seal the bags tightly before shaking.)

4. Taking care not to touch the rigatoni, dump it out to dry on sheets of newspaper. Air drying will take about a day. If you're in a hurry (and, of course, kids usually are), the beads will bake dry in just two minutes on an aluminum foil-covered cookie sheet in a 200° oven.

Day Two (or Perhaps Only Minutes Later)

1. Help the kids measure out lengths of yarn for necklaces, bracelets, or headbands (leave a little extra to tie a knot) and then cut them with scissors. Knot one end around a pencil right away to keep beads from slipping off as the kids work.

YOU'LL THANK YOURSELF LATER

If you must handle wet beads when making pasta jewelry, use plastic gloves or other protection to avoid getting food coloring on your hands—it won't wash off easily.

2. Show your kids how to thread their pasta beads onto the yarn.

3. Help them finish their jewelry by tying the free ends together.

PASTE THE PASTA, PLEASE

Wondering what to do with unstrung pasta from your jewelry project? Stop by a craft store and pick up some cheap wooden picture frames. Let your child glue the leftover pieces in decorative patterns to cover the wood. The more the better!

HUMPTY-DUMPTY MOSAICS

Your kids will be crowing for more when you show them the idea you've hatched this time—eggshell art! It's easy and it consumes their interest (and their time). You'll need:

Eggshells

Brightly colored construction paper

Washable markers

Craft glue

1. Wash, dry, and save the eggshells every time you serve or cook with eggs.

2. When your child is in the mood for an art project, have him draw a large design on a sheet of construction paper—a dinosaur, perhaps, or a prowling tiger.

3. Next have your child color the eggshell pieces with washable markers, using shades he'd like to appear in his design. (He'll find it easier to color large eggshell chunks rather than small ones.)

4. When the coloring is done, let your child break the eggshells into smaller pieces.

5. Using his palette of colored fragments, he now can glue them in place to form his mosaic. Voilà! A work of great eggs-actitude!

SOFT ART

Most kids get nearly as much delight from feeling the textures of the materials they work with as they do from making the art itself. Perhaps that explains why they love working with soft, fluffy cotton balls.

For obvious reasons, your little artists will get the best results if they choose subjects that are naturally white. You might suggest that they make a woolly lamb, a bunny, a ghost, a moonscape, clouds, a poodle, a snowman, an igloo, an arctic fox, or a polar bear.

Other possibilities for more advanced artists include using the cotton sparingly in a scene featuring snow—for example, a fir tree with snowy boughs or a cottage with a snow-covered roof. The nonwhite parts of the drawing can be colored with markers or crayons or can even be built from appropriately colored paper shapes pasted in place.

For the laziest form of cotton-ball art, you'll need:

Construction paper

Washable markers or crayons

Craft glue

A bag of cotton balls

1. Have your child begin by drawing a big design on a sheet of brightly colored construction paper.

2. Next let her fill in the shape with glued-on cotton balls to make a fluffy, puffy picture.

3. Let older children use markers or crayons to add detail to nonwhite parts of the work, or they might want to add colored paper scraps.

4. For some fun variations, your child might glue down kernels of candy corn to make a Halloween pumpkin or red and green M&M's to make a Christmas wreath or tree.

EASY ART ON A ROLL

Many brands of paper towels feature outline drawings of animals, flowers, hearts, and holiday themes that just beg to be colored. The next time you need an instant art project, tear off a few decorator paper towels and grab a handful of crayons. (That's all!)

Encourage the kids to color in the designs so you can use their finished artwork as fancy dinner napkins. (This

QUICK ●II● PAINLESS

If your child is working on a candy mosaic, make sure you provide more than enough candy. We've noticed that most young artists require extra "paint" because there's a tendency for some of it to wander into the mouth.

can be a big hit with grandparents at family get-togethers such as Thanksgiving.) There's also another big plus. You'll be amazed by how cheerfully your kids will set the table when their own masterpieces are involved.

"ALL ABOUT ME" BOOKS

Once a year, perhaps on their birthdays, have each of your kids make a keepsake book that documents their life at that point. Give them blank sheets of paper with headings such as My Favorite Foods, My Best Friends, My Pets, My Biggest Gripes, and My Favorite Sports. Also include a blank introductory page with a heading that reads "A Letter to Myself at Age 12" (or any other age).

Encourage your kids to write and decorate the pages of their book however they want. Don't let them forget to design a cover. When they're finished, have them punch a series of equally-spaced holes down the left-hand margins so they can "sew" the pages together with colored yarn.

SPIRIT ROCKS

Have you ever puzzled over a rock the way a sculptor does, searching for the form hidden inside? Many Native Americans believe rocks are sacred because they contain such spirit forms. To begin this art project, send your little rock hounds outside with instructions to collect an assortment of palm-sized stones.

When the foragers come clanking back, help them wash, dry, and study each find. What does it look like? A sailboat? A frog? A favorite "rock" star?

IF YOU'RE SO
INCLINED

Give your child a snapshot of herself to use on the cover of her "All About Me" book. If you have photos of her room, her best friends, and so on, let her use these as well.

When your kids "see" a shape in a rock, encourage them to bring it to life by adding details with washable tempera paint. One child we know had so much fun painting a lumpy hippo that he went on to make a whole petroglyphic zoo!

FREE-FORM SCULPTURES

The next time you receive something in the mail protected with biodegradable packing peanuts (the kind that melt in water because they're made from vegetable starch), round up your crew for a fun, modern art project. You'll need:

Newspaper

Biodegradable packing peanuts

A small bowl

Tap water

A big spoon

A small paintbrush for each child

1. Spread newspaper on the table to protect the work surface.

2. Dump out a mound of packing peanuts for your little sculptors to work with.

3. Put several of the peanuts in a small bowl and add a couple spoonfuls of water.

4. Let your kids take turns squishing the peanuts into the water with the spoon. They'll be amazed to see the peanuts dissolve! Keep adding peanuts until you have a thick paste.

QUICK ⬤ PAINLESS

A "memory stick" is an easy project for two friends. Let each child find a thick stick and paint it with bold bands of color using washable tempera paints. Next let them add dots of paint, squiggly lines, and so on. When the sticks are dry, the kids can exchange them as a memory of their friendship.

5. With the help of a paintbrush dipped in melted peanuts, let your kids "glue" the remaining packing peanuts together. They can make DNA strands; strange, stiff necklaces; spiky snowballs; space stations; knobby-stick men; free-form sculptures—there's no end to the possibilities!

6. If your kids run out of glue, they'll enjoy making some more.

LEAFY STATIONERY

Although this project can be done with almost any paper, using unusual colors and textures will add a professional-looking touch. Most printers will gladly give you their leftover paper scraps from printing jobs, and they sometimes toss in outdated paper samples as well. By collecting these discards, you'll soon assemble a variety of textures and colors—perfect for your kids to use in making handmade bookmarks, note cards, and gift tags.

For leafy paper art, you'll need:

Autumn leaves

Waxed paper

Large, heavy book

Suitable paper scraps

Scissors

Craft glue

Raffia ribbon (optional)

1. In the fall, challenge your child to go outside and collect as many different shapes and colors of leaves as he can find. (This in itself can keep a kid entertained for a long time!)

2. Press the leaves in a heavy book between sheets of waxed paper. Allow several days for the leaves to flatten.

3. Have your child rummage through your box of paper scraps to find pieces suitable for bookmarks, note cards, or gift tags. Have him trim the paper to size, if necessary.

4. Next let him choose autumn leaves to glue onto the paper—a series of small, colorful leaves on a bookmark, perhaps, or a large maple leaf on a card.

5. If he's making a set of note cards to give as a gift, show him how to tie a half-dozen together with a rustic raffia bow.

FIZZY PAINT

Most kids love the chance to dabble with water colors, especially if you let them make their own. We like the following recipe for homemade water colors because of the fizz factor. You'll need:

2 tablespoons vinegar

2 tablespoons baking soda

2 tablespoons cornstarch

QUICK 🔲 PAINLESS

Pressed autumn leaves add a festive touch to a Thanksgiving table. Have your kids gather and press some leaves ahead of time. When the big day comes, let them arrange a pristine leaf on each plate.

1 tablespoon corn syrup

A mixing bowl

A spoon for stirring

A separate container for each color

Food coloring

Six small plastic bottle caps

Sturdy paintbrushes

1. Stir the vinegar and baking soda together to make a nice, fizzy mixture.

2. When the fizzing stops, add the cornstarch and corn syrup and then swoosh it all together.

3. Divide the resulting cake-like mixture into the six bottle caps.

4. Using a paintbrush, stir a few drops of food coloring into each cap. (In addition to the four basic colors in the box of food coloring, remind your kids that yellow and red make orange and that blue and red make purple.)

5. Your kids can work with their paints now, or they can wait until later. They just need to use a wet paintbrush to bring the colors to life.

STICK 'EM UP!

Here's a concoction that will stamp a grin across every kid's face—lickable glue. With this stuff, kids can turn anything they draw into a classy stamp or sticker.

QUICK 🏁 PAINLESS

Give your kids a handful of craft sticks and some washable markers and let them make stick puppets. They'll have fun drawing silly faces and clothes— and might even decide to stage a puppet show.

To make some, here's what you'll need:

One packet (¼ ounce) unflavored gelatin

A ceramic bowl

¼ cup boiling water

1 tablespoon sugar

¼ teaspoon of a favorite flavoring or a few drops of
  peppermint oil

1. Have one of your kids pour the gelatin into the
   bowl.

2. Gently add the boiling water (make sure you do this
   yourself) and have a helper stir until dissolved.

3. Finally, mix in the sugar and flavoring.

4. Allow the mixture to cool and then brush it onto
   paper as a scrumptious, lickable glue. Here are some
   crafty ideas:

■ Have your kids draw and cut out stickers or stamps
  and then back them with lickable glue.

■ Give your children some old envelopes. Let them
  squiggle on addresses and add their own stamps.
  They can set up their own post office to cancel and
  deliver the mail.

■ Have your kids write letters to friends or relatives
  using envelopes decorated with their own fancy
  stickers (Kids' Express!, Official Male, Official Femail).
  Tuck in some special stickers for the recipient.

A COMPLETE WASTE OF TIME

The 3 Worst Things to Do
With Lickable Glue Are:

1. Let the kids set their
   freshly-coated stamps
   to dry glue-side down
   on the kitchen table. It
   won't hurt the table,
   but it destroys the
   stamps.

2. Refrigerate leftover
   glue in an old yogurt
   container. The baby-
   sitter is sure to eat it
   and be lulled into sup-
   posing that yogurt is
   actually edible. This is
   probably how many
   yogurt-eaters acquire
   the pernicious habit.

3. Store the kids' lick-
   ables in the same
   drawer with your
   postage stamps. A
   lone toddler can lick
   through 30 dollars
   faster than you can
   say, "Where's Wally?"

■ Have them imagine what stamps from foreign countries might look like. Encourage them to make some for countries such as China and Chile or for our favorites: Kiribati, Tuvalu, and Nauru.

BODY PAINT

From the Age of Mastodons to the Age of Maybelline, body painting has delighted humanity. Kids love messing with it, no matter the season. When they get to make their own paint, it's twice the fun. You'll need:

    1 cup cornstarch

    ½ cup cold cream

    ½ cup water

    A large mixing bowl

    A large spoon

    Food coloring

    A muffin tin

1. Stir the cornstarch, cold cream, and water together in a big bowl.

2. Divide the mixture into individual muffin tins so each color has its own cup.

3. Add food coloring to each cup to make the colors you want.

4. Dip in a finger or a brush and let the fun begin. Here are some crafty ideas:

YOU'LL THANK YOURSELF LATER

Your kids will enjoy using their homemade paint to make watercolor paintings. For an easy cleanup, make sure to spread some old newspapers under their work area.

- Your kids can paint on a wristwatch, a bracelet, rings, a necklace, or even a pair of glasses.

- They can bedeck themselves with war paint, can sprout a set of multicolor polka-dots, can draw on a clown's face, or can morph into a cat with whiskers.

Worried about the mess? Squeaky-clean kids are just a bath away.

QUICK ☐ PAINLESS

Fist faces are fun and are easy to make with body paint. Show your kids how to paint the mouth at the forefinger and the thumb and then make it "talk."

Getting Time on Your Side

	The Old Way	The Lazy Way
Time spent looking for something the kids can color	15 minutes	15 seconds
Number of craft projects needed to fill the day	15	2 minutes
Time spent shopping for the right frame to hold gift photos of the kids	50 minutes	0 minutes
Time spent convincing kids that eggs actually are edible	20 minutes	0 minutes
Time spent getting kids to practice their handwriting by writing letters	40 minutes	0 minutes
Time to yourself	5 minutes	80 minutes

By Hook or by Book, Make Them Love to Read

Actually, you won't even need the hook. Despite what you've heard, it's easy to spark a child's interest in reading. We'll show you how. After that, your kids can entertain themselves almost anytime and anywhere.

A child is never too young to be introduced to the magic of books. Some people's most treasured memories of early childhood are of sitting on a parent's lap for a cozy reading session. Begin with board books for the very young (if they dip 'em in oatmeal, you can wipe off the pages) and then move on to picture books. Early reading not only helps nurture the child-parent bond, it leads your little one to begin associating pictures with words, thus laying the foundation for independent reading.

Even after your kids have learned to read on their own, spend time reading together. Choose books above their

present reading level but not beyond their ability to follow with interest (sorry, Martin Heidegger will have to wait). You also can let them read to you from one of their favorite books.

TIPS FOR THE YOUNGER SET

In addition to reading to your kids when they're small, here are some other suggestions for sparking an interest in books:

- When you read to your child, use different voices for the different characters and read expressively.

- Infrequently, pause to ask what your child thinks is about to happen or what she would have done in a certain situation. Verbalizing an answer helps her formulate her thoughts about the story and increases her sense of participation.

- Make sure the book you chose holds your child's attention. If she shows disinterest in a title, promptly move on to another book (*de gustibus non est disputandum*—there's no arguing over taste).

- If your child loves a particular book, be patient enough to read it again and again.

- In addition to story books, check out the occasional alphabet book to help your little one begin to recognize the letters and their sounds.

- Make sure your child's room has shelves containing books within easy reach—board books for the very young, picture books for the slightly older child. It's always wonderful to walk into the room and see a child "reading." (The process begins with a child thumbing through books and looking at the pictures.)

- Help your child realize that the written word is an important part of life. Read billboards, signs, and instructions out loud.

- Wrap up at least one book for each child on gift-giving occasions.

THE LORE OF BOOK LURING

What if your child knows how to read but just doesn't like to? Match a reluctant reader with a book he really loves, and you'll be treated to a wonderful transformation. The child who couldn't bear to read more than a few pages will suddenly spend his spare time eagerly absorbed in a book.

"Mice are defending the abbey!"

"Pa is lost in a blizzard!"

"Einstein's teacher thinks he's too stupid to learn!"

The secret lies in finding the right title, the one that will lead your kids to discover that books can be exciting and fun. Of course, you might have to abandon your dream that they'll curl up with Homer, James, and Faulkner (though this might come later). If the latest issue of *Hot Rod* magazine is what does the trick, rejoice! A rose is a rose, and reading is reading! Here are some tips for finding that perfect fit:

YOU'LL THANK YOURSELF LATER

Establish a Library Day. Some families might go once a week—a Saturday ritual—while others might go every two weeks. The reliable pattern stresses that reading is important, and it regularly offers children the excitement of discovering something new.

- Ask the most important question, "What most fascinates my child?" Go out and find books, magazines, manuals, or comics that match that interest.

- Bring your child with you on frequent trips to the library or a bookstore. Give him plenty of time to freely explore the shelves. This introduces him to the pleasures of browsing and helps you identify the types of books he likes.

- Make your library or bookstore outings a fun family affair by stopping for ice cream or hot chocolate afterwards.

- Try different categories of books such as mysteries, fantasy, science fiction, humor, and historical fiction. And don't forget that some people prefer nonfiction. If so, give 'em facts.

- Don't be discouraged if the early titles you find don't click. Eventually, something will.

- Ask for recommendations from librarians, book sellers, other parents, and other kids.

- Don't fret over your child's choices. The third grader who contentedly chooses a series like *The Babysitters Club* eventually will move on to meatier fare.

- Keep in mind that magazines, comic books, and cartoon collections often serve as important stepping stones to books.

- When a child finds a book she loves, look for more titles by the same author or in the same genre.

Has your child found a series she loves? Reward her with a trip to the bookstore where she can pick out the next title.

The Lazy Way

THE SUBTLE ART OF RAISING READERS

Fortunately, you can make the written word a natural part of your child's life simply by providing the right environment. Here are some useful suggestions for making your household a fertile ground for readers:

- Continue the tradition of reading to your child long after she's learned to read. Take turns reading, praise her efforts, and talk about the books you read together. Your child will see that you enjoy reading with her, which will give her conclusive proof that reading is fun.

- When your child is eager to hear you read more from a book, encourage independent reading by occasionally claiming you're too tired (yawn) to read anymore that night. Suggest he take the book with him to bed.

- Be a role model. Let your kids see you curled up with a book or absorbed in a magazine. If you encounter an especially witty or profound tidbit in your reading, share it aloud with your child. Your enthusiasm for the word will find its mark, even if the subject matter zings over his head.

- Place your child's favorite reading materials in strategic spots: in the car, in the den, near the kitchen table. Also tuck paperbacks in the Caboodle of Fun described in Chapter 4.

- Show your readiness to buy books. "No, you may not have the chewing gum. Do you want that book?

Sure, put it in the cart." The message your child understands is that books, as much as bread, are staples of life.

- Make sure your house has some comfortable reading areas such as a porch swing, cozy couches and chairs, or even a window seat.

- Make your child's bedroom and the dinner table a TV-free zone.

- Limit TV time. (Even adults benefit when they stop letting their lives be sucked into the glowing vacuum tube every night.)

- Don't bother with clever computer programs that read aloud and reward mouse-clicks with noisy animation. After the glitter fades, they create recipients not readers. A reader is an involved and imaginative magician summoning living worlds from little marks on paper.

- Let your child read in bed without a lights-out rule.

- Make "book talk" part of your dinner conversation. It's fun to discuss books with your child (and it reinforces the importance of reading).

- Take your child to book signings and readings by favorite authors.

- Children's book clubs, organized by some stores and libraries, can be fun as well.

For even more tips about nurturing a love of reading, consult the wonderful books by teacher Mary Leonhardt (listed in Appendix B).

YOU'LL THANK YOURSELF LATER

When your child asks "Why?" go to a book. Look up the subject together. (If he can't yet read or if the text is beyond his reading level, read the answer to him.) He'll soon learn from your example that books are powerful tools that can answer any question.

Finally, remember that—as in all aspects of childhood development—progress occurs haltingly. There often will be glowing advances followed by worrisome backsliding. Your child, who has been avidly reading the *Animorphs* series, might suddenly stop caring about the next installment and prefer to go skating instead. Don't panic. Just quietly keep making sure interesting reading material is around, keep offering to read aloud at bedtime, and keep reading yourself. In a little while, your child will pick up a book again, although it might be an altogether different book such as a biography of a figure skater.

QUICK n PAINLESS

Tuck a gift certificate for books in your child's Christmas stocking and Easter basket. Miniature books are a good idea as well.

Getting Time on Your Side

	The Old Way	The Lazy Way
Time spent worrying that your kids don't read enough	100s of hours	0 hours
Time spent reading to your kids instead of dusting and mopping	0 hours	100s of hours
Time spent helping kids write reports about books they didn't read	100s of hours	0 hours
Time spent worrying about why your kid only wants to read comic books	100s of hours	0 hours
Time spent trying to convince your kid that he should have loved *Treasure Island* as much as you did	10 frustrating hours	0 hours
Time spent feeling guilty because your kids see you reading Amy Tan instead of baking fresh bread	100s of hours	0 hours

Instant Happiness from Household Chores

Do we detect a trace of skepticism on your face? Well, believe it! Your kids will be fighting over who gets to carry out the garbage.

The trick is to employ psychology. As you will see, psychology works for free and is pretty fast, too.

IMAGINE THAT! THEY'RE WORKING!

Hidden inside every child is an actor who loves the world of make-believe. Wise parents (who must, therefore, be *Lazy Way* parents) can tap into this childhood magic to get chores done while everyone has fun.

One of our most successful tricks when a work assignment draws an initial "Aw, do I have to?" is to answer in a character voice. Here are a few of our favorites for you to try. Swap them around, ham it up—but most important of all, have fun. You'll be surprised by how readily your kids respond.

QUICK ●ⅱ● PAINLESS

A favorite movie or book can help motivate your crew. After seeing a movie such as *Antz*, for example, your kids might like to pretend they're worker insects digging into a task.

- Become Neil Armstrong talking to his crew (using a deep voice): "This is Neil Armstrong. What do you mean, Captain Wallace, you don't want to clean up? How will we ever get to the moon in this messy ship? I can't even find the ignition switch."

- Become a football coach pumping up his team (use a gruff voice): "Team, you wanta win, don'tcha? Well, you can't win with a locker room like this! Get this equipment off the floor. Pick up these uniforms! Now, hustle, hustle, hustle! Let's see that muscle!"

- Girls are amused by directions from an Italian movie director: "Actressa, we are aready for to shoot your nexta scene. In disa scene, the royal princessa—datsa you—she hasa disguise herself as a maid. All aroun' you, the enemy soldiers, they are asearchin' while you work right in their midst washin' desa dishes. One falsa step and they may discover that you are not really who you seema to be. Are we ready? Lights! Camera! Action!"

- A mechanical robot is another fun choice: "This-is-your-robot-friend. I-see-clothes-on-the-floor. I-detect-an-unmade-bed. Action-is-needed. Does-this-compute?"

- Taking out the garbage is a perfect job for the Bomb Squad. Your child is given the opportunity to save the day by removing the suspicious bag and putting it into the explosion container.

- Even older kids pay attention to a squeaky plea from a toy left carelessly on the floor. "Hey Sam, this is your toy car! Please pick me up and put me on my shelf! I'm scared someone will step on me and break my wheel."

- If toys can talk, why not clothes? You might feel foolish, at first, turning into a shirt who needs help getting into the hamper, but you'll soon find that it's hilarious fun.

- Inspired by a story like "The Shoemaker and the Elves," your kids might want to pretend they're elves busily cleaning up.

- Become a military sergeant. Have your kids click their heels together and salute when it's time for inspection. "Atten, hut! Prepare for barracks inspection."

- Put on a fake plastic nose and glasses and pretend you're a health inspector. Try out your silliest French accent as you begin "lookeeng for le dust an' ze leetle spider cobwebs."

CHORE UP, THIS WILL BE FUN!

Frankly, household chores need to hire a better spin doctor. They've somehow acquired an image among kids that they are—shall we say—boring, even tedious.

This runs contrary to the whole philosophy of *The Lazy Way* parent that work—even damnable, unavoidable work—is expected to be conducted in a spirit of fun. We'll show you what we mean.

The Great Trash Race

The steady tick of a kitchen timer can send kids off and running, eager to do chores. Can they clean the hall

YOU'LL THANK YOURSELF LATER

The next time you're at the grocery store, pick up a cheap kitchen timer that ticks through every passing second like a cartoon time bomb. You'll find it much more motivating than the discreetly silent ones built into most ovens.

bathroom before the buzzer sounds? Can they haul the trash to the curb in record time?

The first time you instigate a timer challenge, have your child estimate how long the task will take and then see if he can beat it. Keep in mind that it never hurts to add a cheering section. ("Ready, set... Go Ben, go!") Some kids like to record how long a job takes and then try to beat their record (or a sibling's) the next time they tackle that chore.

You might even want to award titles, such as "To Joe, the All-Time Champ of the Great Trash Race!"

The Old Switcheroo

The easiest way to handle housework is to do a little at a time. On occasions when the whole house needs cleaning, however, try assigning each person a room and then setting the timer for 10 or 15 minutes. When the buzzer sounds, everyone must switch. To avoid total chaos, set up a clockwise rotation—from the kitchen to the dining room, for example, and from the dining room to the living room. Continue rotating rooms until all the work is done.

Quarter Time

Another idea for whole-house cleaning is to hide quarters for your helpers to find. Let your kids know how many are hidden and see who can find the most. Here are some ideas for hiding places: taped to the inside cover of the hamper, placed on top of an unmade bed, or set on a dresser thick with dust. The job must be

Remind your crew that doing a little housework every day is much less daunting than tackling the whole house at once. Involve your kids in a 10-minute cleanup session every day, perhaps before bedtime. (To add a little fun, blow a whistle and let the work begin!)

completed, of course, before the finder can keep the change. ("Aw, gee, no fair!")

Chinese Style

A little silliness never hurts when it comes to housework. Surprise your kids by passing out tongs or chopsticks and challenging them to pick up clothes and toys. Add to the fun by trying this yourself while muttering in a Chinese accent: "Ah, so! Velly hard to pick up toy with chopstick!"

Ye Olde Treasure Hunte

That old standby, the treasure hunt, never fails to appeal to kids. You'll need:

Paper slips with clues

Tape

A homemade reward coupon

1. Start your kids by handing them the first clue, which will lead them clue-by-clue (complete with instructions) to each job that needs doing. The first clue, for example, might read "Look in the hamper."

2. The second clue (found taped inside the cover of the hamper) might then read "Put these clothes in a basket and take them to the laundry room."

3. The third clue (found on top of the clothes dryer) might follow with "The mystery continues in your room when you make your bed."

4. At the end of the trail, reward your kids with a coupon for homemade cookies or whatever else you might deem appropriate.

When the house looks great thanks to helping hands, celebrate by rounding up the kids for a surprise trip to the movies.

The Lazy Way

Music Makers

Most adults know that playing upbeat music can help make housework a lot more fun, but kids will find it a novel idea. Try putting on some reggae or calypso music and see what happens. Can everyone finish their work before the last song ends and the dreaded opera singing begins? Arghhhh! Cover your ears!

Money Talks

In addition to your child's everyday chores, you might want to create a list of extra jobs such as washing the car or mowing the grass. Next to each task, jot down the wages you'll pay to the enterprising kid who does the work. Some parents even post "Want Ads" on a family bulletin board to advertise available chores.

> "Needed: one hard-working kid to... write this book."

> (Well, we can't promise that this tactic always works!)

ALL HANDS ON DECK

Most kids find doing chores a snap if everyone in the family pitches in—including you. Mention that the whole family will do something fun when the cleanup is over, and they'll whistle as they work (if they can figure out how).

The Great Sock Match

It's no secret that kids love competition. Dump out the sock drawer and see who can match the most pairs. "Ready, set, sock it to 'em!"

IF YOU'RE SO
INCLINED

It never hurts to reminisce about the old days and your childhood chores: getting up to milk the cows at 5am, helping Ma light the fire, and so on. (Well, okay, it wasn't that bad—so why don't you just read your children some books about pioneer days?)

"And the winner is, the amazing, the talented... Amy!"

Job Jars

Remember the job jars from Chapter 10? They work equally well for indoor chores. As before, make sure each task is brief, preferably no more than 15 minutes worth of work. If necessary, break a large task into smaller parts.

You can make pulling a task from the job jar a getting-home-from-school tradition (a way to earn that after-school snack), or you can make it an occasional Saturday morning event for the whole family. You'll need:

Slips of paper with short tasks for kids and adults

A job jar for kids

A job jar for adults

1. Place the job slips in the appropriate jars.

2. With a dramatic flourish, put your hand inside the kids' jar and pull out and read a task for each child.

3. Next let your kids choose a job for you.

4. Make your kids laugh by acting as though you're stuck with a really gruesome chore. "Oh, no! I have to scrub the tub? Are you sure that's what it says? I hate to scrub the tub!"

5. Continue drawing tasks for each other until, well, you're tired of doing work like scrubbing the tub.

When your child wants to invite a friend over, you can agree by saying "Sure, after you've [fill in the blank with a small task]."

6. To add to the element of surprise, include a Wild Card slip in the kids' job jar that enables them to choose their own task. You can even append a suggestion to make it a more pleasant task, if you like. "Wild Card! Choose any task you want—and this includes cleaning the cake plate by eating the last piece and then putting the plate in the dishwasher."

Freedom of Choice

If you give your kids flexibility in setting the table, they'll approach the job with less groaning (and, sometimes, no groaning at all). Set the ground rules clearly. They can set the table any way they want, but they must provide each person with the basics.

You'll probably all enjoy the quirky dinner tables that result. Ours have ranged from a toy Godzilla centerpiece to a table replete with candles, a dandelion bouquet, hidden napkins, and upside-down plates.

IN THE GROCERY STORE

Wish you had some help instead of restless behavior in the grocery store? Here are some ideas for a stress-free trip down the aisles:

- If your kids are old enough, give each child some coupons and send them on a scavenger hunt. Who can find the right brand of crackers? Of yogurt? Of soup?

- Slip in a little math by letting your kids weigh fruits and vegetables in the produce section. After they've had some practice, add to the fun by seeing who can most closely guess how much a choice will weigh.

- Some kids like the job of adding up prices as you shop. Give them a calculator and let them key in the numbers as you make your way down the aisles. If the child is especially adept at arithmetic, dispense with the calculator.

- Let each child choose two or three items to add to your grocery cart, but first explain the rules. Whatever they choose must be sugar-free (or preservative-free, or whatever freedom you seek). The idea is to get the kids in the habit of reading labels.

- When they're ready, entrust them with the job of steering the cart. Make a ceremony of it. It's a major rite of passage in everyone's life.

- Toddlers get a kick out of pushing the small plastic grocery carts provided by some stores. If your store doesn't have them, you still can supply entertainment by letting them "start up" the cart by pushing the "button" on top of a conveniently-placed can or jar. Whoa! They've got to press it to stop, too.

IF YOU'RE SO
INCLINED

Toddlers also can help "steer" the grocery cart by using the plastic top of a family-size can of coffee placed between their legs as the steering wheel.

Getting Time on Your Side

	The Old Way	The Lazy Way
Daily time spent getting kids to do their household chores	10 minutes	3 minutes
Number of chores you end up doing anyway	2	0
Number of angry words	12	0
Time wasted in the grocery store finding and herding kids	15 minutes	0 minutes
Record time for cleaning the hall bathroom	18 minutes	6 minutes and 15 seconds!
Supervision of moaning workers as they clean their room	2 hours	0 hours

Presto Pesto! Kids in the Kitchen

When hunger strikes, all roads lead to the range. This means the kids will be in the kitchen with you, so you might as well have a little help with the measuring, pouring, and stirring. Here are some imaginative ideas, recipes, and guidelines to help you and your kids whip up some fun.

YOUNG CHEFS

In addition to preventing unsupervised mayhem in the next room, involving little hands with cooking provides your kids with many positive benefits. Cooking from a recipe gives them practice following directions and helps teach them the importance of planning ahead. Younger children get to practice valuable physical skills and experience the pride of being useful.

Being a *Lazy Way* parent means you know the kids can help you with all that counting and weighing, and they can do the math to turn "serves 8" into "serves 5." You can send a kid to the dictionary to find out what "brochette" means and then have her search the kitchen to see if you have one. By the time the food is ready, she'll have burned up many mental calories and will be extra hungry. Still, most parents agree that the ultimate reason to have kids in the kitchen is that it's fun!

Use a Potful of Common Sense

A working kitchen will likely be filled with things that get red hot, that splatter without warning, that boil over violently, that roar at an accidental touch, and that grind or slice viciously whatever they encounter. Somewhere in and amongst the frivolity, *The Lazy Way* parent always manages to keep the kids carefully supervised. Here are some of the more important common-sense precautions to get you started:

- Always supervise the kids—every minute, all of the time.

- Make sure both you and the kids wash your hands before handling food (and after every finger-licking). No tasting from a spoon and then sticking it back in the bowl, either.

- Have everyone (including you) wear short or tight-fitting sleeves and an apron.

- Keep all electrical appliances unplugged when not in use and only let adults or responsible teens use them.

- Keep kids away from the stove and the oven.

- Always turn your pot handles to the side to prevent accidentally causing a disastrous hot spill.

- Be sure every kid knows not to touch a hot pot.

- Keep knives—and other things little kids might find tempting to grab—out of reach and, even better, out of sight.

- Don't let anyone rub their eyes after handling onions or hot peppers. A few of the hottest peppers are so strong that children can be affected by capsicum absorbed through their skin.

Age-Appropriate Tasks

Here is a general guide to help you think about which tasks your kids might try. You know your child's development best; don't feel your child should do something just because he's a certain age. Development of physical skills very commonly leads or trails the "average" by a large time span. Until at least age 30, one of the authors was a danger to himself and others in the kitchen, and he's got some scars to prove it.

Preschool

- Stir ingredients together in an extra big bowl
- Stand by to add premeasured ingredients
- Wash vegetables or fruits in a big bowl
- Use a pizza cutter to cube soft bread for croutons
- Tear prewashed lettuce for salads

IF YOU'RE SO INCLINED

Add a few giggles to kitchen tasks by talking in a funny French accent as you "tear zee lettuce" and "stir zee soup." Magnifique!

- Wipe the table or the kitchen counter
- Knead bread dough
- Twist cut lemons or limes on a manual juicer
- Use a manual eggbeater with eggs or liquid batters

1st and 2nd Graders

- Fill measuring cups and spoons
- Mix ingredients with a wire whisk or a big spoon
- Put out the silverware and the plates
- Cut up soft foods with a table knife or a plastic knife

3rd and 4th Graders

- Handle the microwave with supervision
- Make simple recipes on their own
- Use a can opener

5th and 6th Graders

- Use the oven with supervision
- Use a grater for shredding ingredients
- Use a chef's knife with close supervision
- Use a potato peeler with close supervision

HANDLING A KITCHEN FULL OF HELP

There you are, elevated to the role of Master Chef with a kitchen full of bouncing, wide-eyed apprentices. They all are eager to start doing something. Right now.

Every *Lazy Way* parent should know how to treat minor burns. (We're worried about you, too, not just the kids.)

1. Remove affected rings or tight clothing before any swelling starts.

2. Run cold water over the burn for 10 minutes.

3. Cover it with a sterile bandage—no ointment or goop of any kind.

4. Take acetaminophen to help reduce pain and swelling.

5. Whatever you did, don't do it again!

The Lazy Way parent had better have a plan or... you know the old saying about too many cooks. Here are some suggestions for putting your pint-sized helpers to work:

- Let an apprentice chef fetch spices and other ingredients from the pantry. Kids also are perfect for getting pots and pans from counter cabinets when necessary. They don't even have to lean over to look inside.

- Have one child line up all the seasonings in order of use.

- Put meatloaf ingredients in a large, sealable plastic bag. Let your child mush everything together by kneading through the bag.

- When baking a pie, let your child make her own small pastries with leftover dough. Show her how to shape them into round balls and then poke a dab of jam into the center.

- For a healthy side dish, have your child carefully push grapes, chunks of pineapple, orange slices, and other pieces of fruit onto wooden skewers. (Cheese cubes can be added as well.)

- Tearing lettuce for a big salad is fun. Kids also like to add the carrots, cucumbers, and other colorful goodies you've sliced. Older kids can do the slicing for you.

- Slip in a little math by having your child help with doubling or halving a recipe. This is especially useful for directions with fractions. ($\frac{3}{4}$ Cup – $\frac{1}{2}$ Cup= ? Mm-hm, that's why we like kids doing the math.)

A COMPLETE WASTE OF TIME

The 3 Worst Things to Do With Kids in the Kitchen Are:

1. Leave them alone with bubbling pots, a hot oven, and plugged-in appliances. Everyone's goose will be cooked pronto.

2. Let them watch at your elbow while you put chicken parts into the fry oil.

3. Use the last paper towel in the house just before they join you in the kitchen. (You're nodding your head. This has happened to you before, hasn't it?)

The next time you fill seal-able plastic bags with left-overs for the freezer, have a junior chef help by writing the name of the food and the date on the outside of the bag.

- Stirring anything 25 times (or whatever number you choose) usually is undertaken with great seriousness and is good counting practice.

- Mashing is always just plain fun for kids. When you're making mashed potatoes, let a helper squish them for you with a hand masher.

- Many older kids enjoy the challenge of making radish roses, swan napkins, and other decorative items.

- Older kids also like cool tools such as garlic presses, hand juicers, whisks, and apple corers.

KEEPING LITTLE HELPERS BUSY

Here are some tried-and-true ways to keep the smallest helpers busy while *The Lazy Way* parent—or a frenzied one—rushes about making dinner.

Little Cook's Bubbling Pot

Have one of the older kids squirt dish-washing detergent (or bubble soap) into a plastic tub or a huge bowl. Blast lukewarm water from the sink sprayer to fill the tub with bubbles. Decant all but about 3 inches of water and set this bubbly delight on the floor in a spot well out of harm's way. You might want to cut a garbage bag open and spread it underneath. Give your toddler some cups, a funnel, and some big spoons. He'll happily slave over his bubbling pot for a gratefully long time.

Stir, Rattle, and Pour

Give a young child a large bowl of dry rice or beans, and she'll dig right in with her hands, reveling in the way it feels. Add a few simple kitchen tools such as plastic cups, big spoons, and small bowls, and she'll stay absorbed until dinnertime.

Sifting

A hand-sifter can help a child build fine-motor skills. Set out a big bowl, pour some flour into the sifter, and let your little one work away. Don't be surprised if he wants to sift again and again.

Fun in the O-Zone

Cheerios are more than predinner snacks for tiny tummies that just can't wait any longer. Kids can have great fun playing with a bunch of little Os. Here are a few ideas:

- Give your child a pair of tweezers, an empty container, and a bowl of dry Cheerios. Show her how to use the tweezers to pick up the Cheerios—one by one—and transfer them to the container.

- If your little one has learned to count, pour some dry Cheerios into a glass jar and have her estimate how many there are. Then pour the lot onto the table so she can tally them up. Show her how to arrange the little circles in rows of five to make the counting easier. (Bigger kids like to do this, too.)

Kids love being appointed Official Tasters. Does the dish need more salt? A little more cheese? Young chefs are flattered to know their opinions count. (But perhaps you'd better taste, too.)

The Lazy Way

- Supply your child with a sheet of construction paper, school glue, and Cheerios so she can make "cerealistic" art. Show her how she can arrange the pieces in the shape of a house, a Cheshire cat, or whatever your young Salvador Dalí imagines.

The Kitchen Cupboard

Pots and pans are favorite toys for toddlers, but chefs can become exasperated when their best skillet is dragged onto the floor and filled with dozens of tiny pebble "beans." An easy solution is to stock one cupboard with old or garage-sale items and make it your child's. That way, your junior chef can bang away with her own pots while you concentrate on dinner.

RECIPES FOR KIDS

Here are a few simple yet tasty recipes that are just right for kids. They're so easy, even Dad could probably make them.

Yabadaba Yams (Serves 6)

It's simple. It's good. It's how every vegetable should taste… and yams are better for you than potatoes. You'll need:

A 9 × 13 baking pan

Aluminum foil

Two 16-oz. cans of yams in syrup

½ cup pecans (other nuts can be used)

QUICK ☜☞ PAINLESS

If you're up to your elbows in a complicated recipe, keep your child busy by letting him make dessert. Have him cut some slice-and-bake cookies with a plastic knife and arrange them on a baking sheet.

⅓ cup brown sugar

One 8-oz. bag of petite marshmallows

1. Ask your parents to turn on the oven and set it to 350°.

2. Pour both cans of yams into the baking pan.

3. Sprinkle the nuts and brown sugar in a tasty layer all over the yams.

4. Loosely cover the pan with a sheet of aluminum foil.

5. Have a grownup put the pan into the oven (on the center rack) and turn on the timer for 30 minutes.

6. When the timer rings, have a grownup remove the hot pan from the oven and lift off the hot aluminum foil.

7. Sprinkle marshmallows all over the yams.

8. Have an adult put the uncovered pan back into the oven to brown for 5 minutes. The yams are ready. It's time to eat!

Chicken à la Pauper (Serves 4)

Here's a tasty main course that is fun to make. You'll need:

An oven-proof pan

A large bowl

Ritz (or similar) crackers (one full sleeve)

One can Cream of Chicken soup

When you and the kids want to cook up a special treat, turn to what arguably is the most popular cooking invention to come out of the 1950s—instant brownie mix. Not to be a name dropper, but we think Betty Crocker is the best choice for kids because the cooking instructions are all in pictures.

The Lazy Way

12 oz. sour cream

½ lb. leftover chicken (or canned chicken)

1. Ask your parents to turn on the oven and set it to 350°.

2. Tear the chicken into little bits (if it isn't already).

3. Here's the fun part. Using your hands, crumble all the crackers into a bowl. Yeah! Crush 'em to bits!

4. Sprinkle the bottom of the pan with a few crushed crackers.

5. Pour the sour cream, soup, and chicken into the cracker bowl and mix.

6. Pour and spread the mixture evenly across the pan.

7. Have a grownup put the pan into the oven to bake for 20 minutes.

8. Voilà! You've cooked the main course for dinner.

3–2–1 Malted Milk (Serves 1)

Here's an easy way to turn an old standby into a special treat that even packs some extra nutrition. You'll need:

Malt powder

Chocolate mix powder

Ground cinnamon

Milk

1. Add 3 teaspoons of malt powder to a 12-oz. glass.

2. Add 2 teaspoons of chocolate mix.

YOU'LL THANK YOURSELF LATER

It's easy to get distracted when cooking with kids. To help keep track of where you are, line up all the ingredients on a tray before you start working. After an item has been used, set it aside. This will keep you from adding salt twice(!) or forgetting the coriander.

3. Add 1 shake of ground cinnamon.

4. Pour just a bit of milk into the bottom of the glass.

5. Stir until the mixture makes a smooth syrup.

6. Fill the glass with milk and stir a bit more.

7. For extra fun, float a spritz of whipped cream dusted with cinnamon when you serve this to your friends.

YOU'LL THANK YOURSELF LATER

Keep a small first-aid kit right in the kitchen. It should contain sterile gauze in various sizes, bandage tape, Band-Aids, providone iodine ointment (it's sting-less!), an antibiotic oint-ment, and (just in case) smelling salts for Mom.

Getting Time on Your Side

	The Old Way	The Lazy Way
Time spent stirring, pouring, and fetching in the kitchen	5 minutes daily	1 minute
Time spent scraping charcoal off pans because a crash from the living room distracted you	10 minutes	0 minutes
Number of times you giggled while cooking dinner	0	3–5
Time spent reading the recipe while one hand stirs in the stuff you shouldn't have added yet	5 minutes	0 minutes
Time spent stooping and bending to fetch pots from the counter cabinets	3 minutes	0 minutes
Total time spent cooking	55 minutes	49 minutes

Chapter
seventeen

Painless Fun for
a Sick Child

Just a few simple props will help keep your child
quiet and content to stay in bed, just like the doctor ordered.

A LITTLE PAMPERING

There's no denying that kids don't struggle too hard to avoid
the occasional sick day. They are happy to be unexpectedly
released from didactic drudgery to lounge about in pajamas
while the world trudges on outside: dogs bark, the school bus
stops at the corner, and the postman makes his rounds. Sure,
there's that sore throat or fever to contend with but, with a
little pampering, even that's not too bad. In fact, some of our
coziest childhood memories stem from sick days.

The Feeling Better Box
The Feeling Better Box described in Chapter 3 is our most powerful prescription for cheering up young patients. If you hold
fast to the rule that the box only appears when your child is

ill, you'll maintain its magic and its mystery. Depending on your choice of contents, recuperating kids can while away their sick day by:

- Poring over mysterious foreign stamps or coins
- Shaking a snow globe to create a wintry scene
- Playing simple card games
- Making faces in a hand mirror
- Trying on costume jewelry
- Arranging stamps or coins in a collector's notebook
- Dabbing on sweet perfume
- Reading a miniature book
- Stringing beads on yarn
- Looking through old photographs
- Entertaining themselves with a book of riddles or jokes
- Marshaling toy soldiers in the hills and valleys of the bedclothes

Half the fun for a child, of course, is digging through the box to rediscover old treasures—and to find out whether new ones have been added since last time. (What? They haven't? Toss in a magnet and some paper clips or a handful of pipe cleaners on your way to the poor child's room!)

The Hand Bell

Make sure your Feeling Better Box contains a hand bell. A bedridden child takes comfort and reassurance from knowing that a parent is just a ring away.

QUICK ◖🕮◗ PAINLESS

For extra fun, respond like an English butler when your child rings his hand bell. "Here is your toy dinosaur. Will that be all, sir?"

KEEP YOUR KIDS BUSY The Lazy Way

A Special Tray

Patients of all ages enjoy the luxury of having meals served to them on a bed tray. Your best choice for a mess-free dining experience is the kind with legs. (Expecting a sick child to balance a tray on his lap is making a feverish bid for trouble.)

A small bouquet of flowers—even dandelions from the yard—will help make the meal a special occasion. Perhaps the best touch of all, however, is to prepare one very special sick-day dish. It's an edible message that unmistakably says "I love you." Here are some ideas:

- That classic comfort food, chicken soup (cluck loudly as you bring it down the hall)

- Milk toast sprinkled with brown sugar and—who cares about cholesterol?—a delicious little dab of melted butter

- Old-fashioned toad-in-a-hole (kids love the name)

- Coddled eggs mixed with crumbled saltines (to soak up all the runny stuff so the kids never know it was there)

- Rice or tapioca pudding with a big smile made of raisins

- An antifever popsicle served in a bowl (to help contain any melting)

Every family quickly finds its own favorites. If you faithfully preserve these sick-day traditions, your kids will remember them with fondness even as their hair grays.

A COMPLETE WASTE OF TIME

The 3 Worst Things to Include on a Bed Tray Are:

1. A cup without a top. Just one little wriggle makes it a cup without contents.

2. A hefty serving of spinach or any other yucky stuff that's sold to the gullible as being "good for you."

3. Math homework tucked into the tray's side pocket. It could easily add several days to an illness.

"Hospital" Menu

To help revive a flagging appetite and to make staying in bed more fun, let your child order meals from a "hospital" menu. On a sheet of paper, jot down a selection of soups, main dishes, and drinks and let your child circle the ones that sound most appealing.

The Reading Corner

Nothing soothes children more than having an adult read to them when they're feeling ill. Even older kids enjoy the luxury of settling down with a parent to hear them read a good book, especially one a bit beyond their own reading level. Here are some tips for sharing books with your kids on sick days:

- Read with dramatic flair and have fun. Try giving different voices to each of the book's characters. Don't rush. The ear is slower than the eye, plus you need time to glance ahead so you know which character voice to use. Sound effects are a delight to children. Let the wind howl and the stairs c-r-e-a-k.

- If your child knows how to read, ask if she'd like to take turns reading with you.

- Most older kids enjoy richly detailed books such as *The Wind in the Willows*, *Redwall*, *The Hobbit*, or *The Lion, Witch and The Wardrobe*. Whatever you end up reading, make sure it's a choice your child wants to hear. (Save *A Brief History of Time* for your own sick days.)

YOU'LL THANK YOURSELF LATER

Reserve a special cup, plate, and bowl that emerge from the cupboard only when your child is ill. If possible, select dishes preserved from the patient's own toddlerhood because of the fond memories already attached. Otherwise, buy a special set with a storybook theme or a detailed illustration.

As you no doubt already know, preschoolers have an endless appetite for picture books. They often want to hear their favorites again and again.

Special Effects

The warm glow of Christmas can comfort sick children, even in July. One considerate mother strings tiny white lights around her daughter's room whenever she is ill. Who wouldn't perk up at the sight of those twinkling lights?

FUN DISTRACTIONS

Aside from all the pampering, kids need things to do when stuck in bed. Here are some of our favorites. Many of the suggestions in Chapter 11 also work well on sick days.

Scrambled Words

It will only take you a minute to make up a list of words for your patient to unscramble. (The real time needed will come on your child's end.) Most kids enjoy the challenge, but it is helpful if words are presented in categories such as sports, animals, states, countries, or foods. Here are some animals to get you started:

- reab (bear)
- nyahe (hyena)
- rigte (tiger)
- eknas (snake)

IF YOU'RE SO
INCLINED

Many libraries now offer books on tape (and on CD) for all ages. Turn to these when your voice gives out or when your 3-year-old wants to hear the same story for the 200th time.

- hsif (fish)

- roshe (horse)

- nilo (lion)

- ethplena (elephant)

Some kids like to unscramble a word and then draw a picture (this works especially well with food and animals) or check it off on a photocopied map (useful with states and countries).

Backward Messages

Evah uoy reve nettirw sdrow sdrawkcab? (Have you ever written words backwards?) Kids usually are amused by how weird this looks. You'll need:

A pencil or pen

Paper

1. Hand your child a piece of paper with a simple backwards message like "I evol uoy" (I love you).

2. Tell him it's a message in code and challenge him to translate it. Give hints, if necessary.

3. When he's figured out the code, give your child a longer message to translate. Double-space each line so your child can write the transcribed words underneath.

4. For an extra challenge, write the message "double backwards," as our son calls it. To do this, also reverse the order of the words. ("I love you" becomes "Uoy evol I.")

5. When your child has decoded your message, let him write a note to you or to a friend.

6. Dluow uoy ekil emos nekcihc puos?

Secret Codes

The idea of creating one's own secret code appeals to most kids. Give your child a pad and a pencil and have her write out the letters of the alphabet and the numbers from 0 to 9 in a long, double-spaced list. Below each letter have her write a different letter or number to create a substitution cipher. (Use check marks to keep track of which letters have been used.) For example, ABC might become 2Z3. Explain to your child that, with her new secret code, she can:

- Share the code with a friend. The two can then exchange notes that no one else can read.
- Write in a private diary.
- Mystify people by using it on book covers.
- Keep birthday and Christmas gifts secret by writing her list in code.

Spotlight

A simple hand mirror and a curious cat can help entertain a sick child. First, show your little scientist how to bounce a ray of light onto the wall. When the beam catches the cat's attention, demonstrate how you can trick it into playing a pouncing game by moving the light around. Even if your household lacks a curious cat, your child will still enjoy making the light dance.

IF YOU'RE SO
INCLINED

If your child takes a special interest in secret codes, look for a book about Egyptian hieroglyphics and let him write a message using the ancient symbols.

Newspaper Re-Do

The curative power of ridiculous giggling, while not yet endorsed by the AMA, is still worth prescribing to every sick child. Especially when it's this easy! You'll need:

Newspapers

A pencil eraser

Washable Markers

1. Give your child some old newspapers.

2. Demonstrate how she can alter the photos with the help of an eraser and markers. She can erase a politician's head, for example, and replace it with a pumpkin—no doubt improving both looks and function. She also can change expressions with the addition of a raised eyebrow, can write a new photo cutline, and can make fun of a pompous bureaucrat by giving him a headband with a drooping feather.

Let her work on her own and then return for a few giggles of your own as she shows you her oddball creations.

Proud of your patient's good behavior? Reward her by renting a favorite movie from the video store and let her prop up on the sofa to watch it.

The Lazy Way

Getting Time on Your Side

	The Old Way	The Lazy Way
Time spent hovering uselessly	2 hours	1 hour
Time spent doing your own projects	0 hours	3 hours
Time spent entertaining at bedside	3 hours	1 hour
Time spent coaxing sausage and sauerkraut on a stay-at-home kid	8 minutes	0 minutes
Time spent bringing requested toys to the bedside	20 minutes	5 minutes
Time spent returning a sick child to bed... again... and again	35 minutes	15 minutes

More Lazy Stuff

How to Get Someone Else to Do It

Many parents complain that two of the most difficult aspects of parenting are hiring good baby-sitters and finding summer activities their kids won't hate. These basic guidelines and simple suggestions should help make both a snap.

The Perfect Sitter

The most wonderful baby-sitter we ever had always showed up with a bright smile on her face and a backpack bulging with fun: big books, little games, even toys. She was entirely self-sufficient and was fully prepared to make boredom or separation anxiety vanish. Although we discovered her through a friend, we knew when she told us she was going off to college that we could never replace her without a thorough and systematic search plan. Here are our best recommendations for finding the best and the brightest baby-sitter.

- If you live in a college town, look for students majoring in early childhood education. They invariably like kids and won't spend the whole evening watching TV.

- Preschools where the principals hire college students as part-time help also can be a good source for baby-sitters. These are most likely located near a university campus. If possible, observe the students in action. You should be able to quickly pick out the ones who really *like* kids.

- Church nurseries often employ high school and college students. Again, watch them in action.

- When your favorite baby-sitter can't make it, ask if she can recommend a friend. Usually, her friend will be good with children as well.

- Some neighborhood associations keep lists of sitters.

- Use networking. When you're at a neighborhood block party, meet other parents at the park, or run into a neighbor while walking the dog, bring up the subject of baby-sitters. Really good ones usually have enthusiastic supporters.

- Observe the older kids in your neighborhood when they are playing with their younger siblings. Perhaps one will stand out as having an especially good rapport with children.

In all cases, ask for references—and check them!

Finding Great Activities

You know about the soccer team, Scouts, and the YMCA/YWCA, but what else is going on? Here are some tips for locating workshops, camps, and classes your kids will enjoy. No matter how great the activities, however, be careful not to pack your child's day with too much to do. All kids need some unstructured time to play, putter, and just be.

- In addition to story time, many libraries offer arts and crafts workshops, readings, and other programs kids enjoy. At our library, for instance, we've heard talks about such diverse subjects as snakes and making kites.

- Local museums can be treasure troves for kids, with fascinating classes about everything from papier-mâché to kitchen chemistry. Some also hold summer camps, and many have special children's museums with interactive exhibits and hands-on activities.

- Nature centers schedule hikes, canoe trips, and workshops with topics such as bird-watching or bats (with craft projects included). Like museums, many nature centers also offer summer camps.

- Aquariums and zoos cater to kids as well, with sleep-overs, special classes, and summer or holiday camps.

- Some kitchen stores offer cooking classes for kids, while arts and crafts stores schedule arts and crafts workshops.

- Many universities arrange special programs for the younger set. Our local university, for instance, has wonderful summer day camps.

- Some theaters and performing arts centers schedule acting classes for kids.

- Your local park system might offer children's programs.

- Check with skating rinks and bowling alleys to see if they offer lessons.

- When looking into a sport, network with other parents. Do they like the coach? The other kids? Is the emphasis on winning or sportsmanship? (We have seen too many red-faced fathers screaming at their frightened kids to dare venture our opinion as to which of these attitudes is better.)

- Check under the Youth Organizations heading in the Yellow Pages. You'll find groups such as the Boys and Girls Clubs and the Catholic Youth Organization. A few quick minutes on the phone can yield a long list of activities for your kids.

B

If You Really Want More, Read These

We think we've covered everything, but it won't hurt our feelings if you still want to read more. We've made a list of helpful books and Web pages you might enjoy.

Books

99 Ways to Get Kids to Love Reading: And 100 Books They'll Love by Mary Leonhardt (Crown Publishing, 1997). A collection of great tips for nurturing a family of readers.

Anna Banana: 101 Jump-Rope Rhymes by Joanna Cole (William Morrow & Co., 1989). More than 100 traditional and funny rhymes to keep those little feet jumping.

The Children's Step-by-Step Cookbook by Angela Wilkes (Dorling Kindersley, 1994). Photographs and easy-to-follow instructions teach older children how to cook.

Children's Traditional Games: Games from 137 Countries and Cultures by Judy Sierra and Robert Kaminski (Oryx Press, 1995). Lets kids travel imaginatively to other lands and climes while playing new and unusual games.

FamilyFun's Crafts edited by Deanna F. Cook (Disney Enterprises, 1997). Jam-packed with great craft ideas for kids such as pine cone ponies, pasta airplanes, coffee can stilts, and ice boats (ice cubes with sails). Also check out *FamilyFun's Games on the Go* by Lisa Stiepock (Hyperion, 1998).

Hopscotch, Hangman, Hot Potato, and Ha, Ha, Ha: A Rulebook of Children's Games by Jack Maquire (Simon & Schuster, 1992). Have you forgotten how to play these childhood favorites? This book will refresh your memory and will teach you some new tricks.

Kids Crazy Concoctions: 50 Mysterious Mixtures for Art & Craft Fun by Jill Frankel Hauser (Williamson Publishing, 1995). From coffee dough to monster magnets, this book is packed with fun ideas.

Kids Create! Art & Craft Experiences for 3- to 9-year-olds by Laurie Carlson (Williamson Publishing). A wonderful collection of easy art projects, including holiday gifts, pop-up cards, and homemade fossils.

Kids Make Music! by Avery Hart and Paul Mantell (Williamson Publishing, 1993). Get ready to clap those hands. Your kids will be singing the dishwashin' blues and picking up toys to rap music.

The Klutz Book of Marbles by Ed Taber (Klutz Press, 1988). All the Klutz books take a light-hearted approach to such diverse topics as magnets, yo-yos, juggling, mazes, and paper airplanes. This one comes packaged with a dozen marbles in a drawstring bag.

Lotions, Potions and Slime: Mudpies and More by Nancy Blakey (Tricycle Press, 1996). From homemade icebergs to crash cookies, the whole family will get a kick out of the imaginative suggestions in this book.

Parents Who Love Reading, Kids Who Don't: How It Happens and What You Can Do About It by Mary Leonhardt (Crown Publishing, 1995). A more detailed book about nurturing a love of reading, by the author of *99 Ways to Get Kids to Love Reading*.

Pretend Soup and Other Real Recipes: A Cookbook for Preschoolers & Up by Mollie Katzen and Ann L. Henderson (Tricycle Press, 1994). A wonderful introduction to cooking with young children featuring lively drawings and simple recipes.

The Read-Aloud Handbook by Jim Trelease (Penguin USA, 4th edition, 1995). A classic that emphasizes the importance of reading to kids and comes complete with a treasury of great children's books.

Science Wizardry for Kids: Authentic, Safe Scientific Experiments Kids Can Perform by Margaret Kenda and Phyllis S. Williams (Barrons', 1992). Let your kids create an electric lemon and make strings sing. Contains more than 200 experiments kids will enjoy.

Tree Houses You Can Actually Build by David R. Stiles (Illustrator) and Jeanie Stiles (Chapters Publishing, 1998). Step-by-step instructions and lots of illustrations make this the definitive book on designing and building tree houses.

Children's Encyclopedias

There are two major multivolume children's encyclopedias. Both are heavily illustrated, reflect contemporary school curricula, and provide hours of enjoyment for children between the ages 7 and 14. They're expensive, so if you can't afford a set for your home, see whether they're available at your local school or library. If they aren't, ask if the library can purchase a set.

- *The New Book of Knowledge* (Grolier Educational, 1997) is a 21-volume, illustrated encyclopedia set that children have read and explored since the first edition was published in 1912. It's arranged by subject, and articles often include activities and experiments.

- *Children's Britannica* (Encyclopaedia Britannica, 1988) is a 20-volume encyclopedia set arranged in the more traditional alphabetical format. Colorful illustrations and graphics and an easy-to-read style engage the young reader's interest.

Web Pages

The Kids on the Web site (www.zen.org/~brendan/kids.html) is a great place to start. It's maintained by Brendan P. Kehoe, who wrote *Zen and the Art of the Internet*. You'll find tons of links to places with fun stuff for kids.

Rather than listing Web pages alphabetically, we decided to rank our list by how much we liked each site.

The Science Museum of Minnesota site (www.sci.mus.mn.us) has a first-class collection of hands-on physics experiments in the Thinking Fountain. We like the ball-bearing soup-can spinner and the parachuting pinwheel best. These are more than just demonstrations of principles, they're fun toys you make yourself!

Nicole's Country Cottage (www.geocities.com/Heartland/Ridge/9865) is a charming personal site created by a young mother of two as a labor of love. Her crafts page leads to a veritable treasure trove of projects for kids culled from the members of Nicole's e-mail discussion list. You are welcome to join the free list yourself, and you'll meet mothers from around the country to share recipes, crafts, and a little tea and sympathy.

The Kid Crafts Bulletin Board (www.wwvisions.com/craftbb/kids.html) is a good place to ask questions, to look for ideas, and to share information about doing crafts with kids.

The Bored Mom (www.cyberus.ca/~cmclaren) is a personal Web site created by a Canadian mother who offers a delightfully humorous look at parenting (check out "Origins of Bored" and "The Hiding Spot") as well as a nice selection of kids' crafts.

KidPub (www.kidpub.org/kidpub) is a site where your kids can upload their stories. It features work by young writers from all over the world.

The site for Michaels Craft Store (www.michaels.com) lists upcoming craft classes and activities. It also contains special pages just for kids along with suggested craft activities.

Bill Nye the Science Guy (nyelabs.kcts.org) lets your kids e-mail questions to their favorite science guy and helps them learn about science. The Home Demos section offers lots of quick and simple home-science projects marred only by some awfully punny titles. Be forewarned, however, that the site is multimedia heavy and, therefore, requires a modern browser with Real Media and Macromedia's Flash. These add-ons can be installed automatically when you visit. Visitors short of disk space or without a sound card and speakers, however, should say "Nay" to Nye.

If You Don't Know What it Means, Look Here

If you've temporarily misplaced the difference between tempera and tempura, this is where you can look it up. (Hint: You can't eat tempera.)

Alien detector   A hand-held gadget that detects aliens, inspired by the movie *Men in Black*.

Alum   Found in the spice department, this powdery substance is most commonly used for making pickles. If you want to sound extra smart, call it a hydrated double salt of aluminum. Yes, you've eaten aluminum!

Anti-Coloring books   Coloring books with deliberate blank spots that prompt children to imagine what they think should have been there and to draw it in themselves. They're published by Henry Holt and are sold in many bookstores.

Box knife   A utility knife designed for cutting cardboard. It features an oversized, replaceable razor that can be retracted into the handle when not in use. It should be used only by adults or responsible teens (is there such a thing?).

Brain Quest cards   A game of 1,000 general knowledge questions printed on slender cards connected like a folding fan. The answers are supplied, so there's no chance you'll be left behind on the floor looking for your brain. They are made by Workman Publishing and are carried by most bookstores.

Caboodle of Fun   A knapsack or duffel bag stocked with goodies to entertain your kids in the car or at the doctor's office.

Character voice   Talking like—"Eh, What's up, Doc?"—Bugs Bunny, or an English lord, or Arnold Schwarzenegger, or the like.

Chinning bar   A metal bar used for doing chin-ups that fits into holders mounted inside a door frame.

Coddled eggs   In an enameled pan, boil enough water so that the top of the eggs will be $\frac{1}{4}$ inch below water. Remove the boiling water from the heat, put in the eggs, cover, and let stand for 8–10 minutes.

Costume box   An invaluable aid to imaginative play. Think of it as a dress-up box—and more.

Craft glue   A sticky, tacky glue available from craft stores. It has the advantage of being less prone to drip.

Crafts bin   The bin where you keep your kids' craft supplies.

Crash corner   A place where kids can "crash" onto a mound of blankets and pillows. A great way to release energy on rainy days.

Dress-up box   See Costume box. (Hah-hah! We've always wanted to do this. Oh… now don't cry. All right, we'll give you a hint: It's full of unusual old clothes.)

Feeling Better Box   A special box filled with toys and other items that your child only gets to enjoy on sick days.

Fireballs   Wads of hand-colored paper used in fast and furious fireball fights. Watch out for the deadly red ones!

Host plants   Plants such as fennel, dill, and passion vine on which caterpillars feed. Without host plants, there would be no butterflies.

Indoor sandbox   A plastic bin filled with sand or cornmeal that can be used for rainy-day play.

Little Guys Box   A large, plastic bin stocked with miniature figures and other tiny stuff. Great for setting up a miniature town or farm.

Milk toast   A simple dish from a simpler time. In a shallow bowl, pour a cup of scalding milk over two slices of heavily buttered crisp toast. Shower with lots of brown sugar. If you have some, plop a slice of crisp bacon on top.

Newspaper broadsheets   The big, wide sheets that are folded down the center to make up four pages of a newspaper.

Newspaper end roll   When the roll of paper feeding into a web press is close to running out, the pressman switches to a new roll by doing a running splice. The old roll, with a small (to a newspaper) bit of paper left, is called the end roll.

Puzzle caddie   A flat caddie on which puzzles can be built and saved. An excellent solution if you have only one table on which to build puzzles.

Rat-A-Tat Cat   No, it's not a game played by John Dillinger with stray cats; it's a card game published by Gamewright that combines memory skills with a bit of poker-like strategy. There's enough skill involved to interest adults, yet it's still within the grasp of most six year olds.

Rigatoni Large, tubular pasta noodles.

School glue The standard white glue usually packaged in small squeeze bottles and sold in the school supplies section of every grocery and drug store.

Schwarzenegger Camp Your own backyard version of a Schwarzenegger workout.

Snow pretzels Candy made by squiggling maple syrup into the snow in the shape of a pretzel.

Squirt paint Craft paint that is gooey but squirtable and that dries on paper in thick, raised lines.

Tempera paint Another name for poster paint. This type of paint is now available as a washable product. This is the stuff that used to be made with egg whites; it's not the stuff you deep fry (tempura).

Tinkering spot A place stocked with art supplies, tools, broken appliances, and other fascinating junk where kids can mess around.

Toad-in-a-hole The classic version goes all the way back to 16th-century England and is what we call "pigs in a blanket," although the British used a biscuit or spoon bread rather than pastry. But we're talking about *Lazy Way* American toads here, so just take a thick slice of buttered bread, whack out the center with a biscuit cutter, and plop the slice buttered-side down onto a hot skillet. Pour a beaten egg into the hole with an optional chunk of sausage for company. Grill one side, brush the top with butter, and flip to grill the other side. Some people also know this as "eggs in a basket."

D

It's Time for Your Reward

After You Do This...	Reward Yourself With This...
Give the kids a fort, a tree house, or a special place.	Close your eyes and remember the look on their faces.
Finish your family's Feeling Better Box.	Have some hot, buttered popcorn while you watch the movie *Wings* starring Gary Cooper and Clara Bow.
Prepare a crafts bin.	You've got more time to yourself. What more could you want?
Stock a costume box with neat stuff.	The comedy to come will keep you in stitches.
Create a science lab/ tinkering spot.	How about that peace and quiet?
Pack up a Caboodle of Fun.	Take the family on a weekend auto trip to test it out.
Learn to play Truth or Lie.	You get a new car. Truth or lie?
Train yourself to always look for the word *washable*.	Now your hands will stop shaking and that nervous tic will go away.

Introduce the kids to shaving cream fun.	Go on, forget the work just this once. Go join 'em!
Plant a butterfly garden.	Your reward will dazzle you.
Make sure every kid has rain boots and a rain suit.	You are finally free of rainy day dread.
Build a wacky snowman and a little snow pet.	Hot chocolates, all around!
Hold your first Pass the Piggy.	Watch the videos you took and giggle all over again.
Set up your first Box City.	That's worth 3–4 hours practically undisturbed.
Remember to save a shoe box, a milk jug, or a toothpaste cap.	Ask the kids for a hug. You deserve it!
Hold your first annual Autumn Celebration.	Enjoy a glass of lemonade on your beautifully clean patio.
Play Job Tag with the family.	You finally got them to help!
Make your first "crash corner."	Have tea and cookies.
Help the kids make paper people.	Invite them to dinner.
Help the kids make invisible ink. (They probably wrote your reward over there somewhere.)	
Make your first Fountain of Foam.	Make another one!
Start the kids on their first Humpty-Dumpty mosaic.	Treat yourself to an egg salad sandwich for lunch.

Bring home a newspaper end roll.

Order pizza 'cause everybody's too busy drawing to help cook.

Make fizzy paint.

Tee-hee-hee-hee!

Hold your household's first Great Trash Race.

Wow. Ice cream all 'round!

Post your first Kid Wanted ad.

The reward comes when the ad gets answered.

Have Yabada Yams with Chicken à la Pauper for dinner.

For this you need a reward? Okay, have seconds.

Index

Now you can do these tasks, too!

The Lazy Way

Starting to think there are a few more of life's little tasks that you've been putting off? Don't worry—we've got you covered. Take a look at all of *The Lazy Way* books available. Just imagine—you can do almost anything *The Lazy Way!*

Clean Your House The Lazy Way
By Barbara H. Durham
0-02-862649-4

Handle Your Money The Lazy Way
By Sarah Young Fisher and Carol Turkington
0-02-862632-X

Care for Your Home The Lazy Way
By Terry Meany
0-02-862646-X

Train Your Dog The Lazy Way
By Andrea Arden
0-87605180-8

Take Care of Your Car The Lazy Way
By Michael Kennedy and Carol Turkington
0-02-862647-8

Cook Your Meals The Lazy Way
By Sharon Bowers
0-02-862644-3

*All Lazy Way books are just $12.95!

additional titles on the back!

Build Your Financial Future The Lazy Way
By Terry Meany
0-02-862648-6

Shed Some Pounds The Lazy Way
By Annette Cain and Becky Cortopassi-Carlson
0-02-862999-X

Organize Your Stuff The Lazy Way
By Toni Ahlgren
0-02-863000-9

Feed Your Kids Right The Lazy Way
By Virginia Van Vynckt
0-02-863001-7

Cut Your Spending The Lazy Way
By Leslie Haggin
0-02-863002-5

Stop Aging The Lazy Way
By Judy Myers, Ph.D.
0-02-862793-8

Get in Shape The Lazy Way
By Annette Cain
0-02-863010-6

Learn French The Lazy Way
By Christophe Desmaison
0-02-863011-4

Learn Italian The Lazy Way
By Gabrielle Euvino
0-02-863014-9

Learn Spanish The Lazy Way
By Steven Hawson
0-02-862650-8